START UP YOUR NONPROFIT LIKE A PRO

Juliana Michael

America Thanking God is proud to dedicate this book to the State of Georgia, which served as our case study throughout its development. As a token of our appreciation, we commit to providing 100 copies, whether in e-copy or hard copy format, annually to newly established nonprofit organizations in the state. We hope this resource will support and inspire these organizations as they embark on their missions to impact our communities positively.

CONTENTS

Title Page
Dedication
Preface:
CHAPTER 1
CHAPTER 2
CHAPTER 3
CHAPTER 4
CHAPTER 5
CHAPTER 6
CHAPTER 7
CHAPTER 8
CHAPTER 9
CHAPTER 10
CHAPTER 11
CHAPTER 12
CHAPTER 13
CHAPTER 14
CHAPTER 15
CHAPTER 16
CHAPTER 17
CHAPTER 18

CHAPTER 19
CHAPTER 20
CHAPTER 21
About The Author   1

Juliana Michael serves as the founder of two operational nonprofit organizations: America Thanking God and Christians in Technology.

©2024 Juliana Michael

All rights reserved. No part of this book may be reproduced or transmitted in any form or by any means, electronic or mechanical, including photocopying, recording, or by any information storage and retrieval system, without permission in writing from the publisher.

ASIN: BOD21P4KF9

Beginning a nonprofit organization demands significant time, commitment, and meticulous planning. Kindly seek legal and regulatory standards for proper legal, accounting, or nonprofit guidance to ensure compliance.

In a constantly evolving landscape where technology is pivotal in our approach to missions and community engagement, nonprofits encounter unprecedented opportunities and challenges. As we navigate this dynamic environment, we must harness innovative tools and strategies to maximize our impact and achieve our organizational objectives.

I extend my deepest gratitude to the Almighty and all who have supported me thus far on this journey. Your unwavering support is invaluable as we strive to make a positive difference.

Several websites serve as practical guides in this book, including:
- https://ecorp.sos.ga.gov/
- https://www.irs.gov/
- https://americathankinggod.org/

"Start Your Non-Profit Like a PRO: The Ultimate Guide to Launching and Running a Successful Non-Profit Organization" - the definitive roadmap to non-profit success that will propel you from novice to expert in record time. In this must-have guide, renowned non-profit strategist Juliana Michael shares her insider secrets and proven strategies for navigating the complex world of non-profit management with confidence and finesse. Whether you're a budding entrepreneur, a passionate advocate, or a seasoned professional, this book is your ticket to unlocking the full potential of your non-profit venture.

With Juliana's expert guidance, you'll learn how to:

Define your mission and vision precisely to attract donors and supporters like never before.

Navigate the legal and regulatory landscape easily, from incorporating your organization to obtaining tax-exempt status.

Build a powerhouse board of directors to drive your non-profit's success and sustainability.

Master the art of fundraising, from crafting compelling grant proposals to cultivating relationships with major donors and corporate sponsors.

Leverage the latest marketing techniques and digital tools to raise awareness, engage your audience, and amplify your impact. Scale your non-profit for long-term growth and scalability while staying true to your mission and values.

Packed with actionable insights, real-world case studies, and practical tips, "Start Your Non-Profit Like a PRO" is your all-in-one resource for launching, managing, and growing a thriving non-profit organization. Take advantage of this opportunity to make a difference in your community and beyond. Order your copy today and join the ranks of successful non-profit leaders changing the world, one mission at a time.

PREFACE:

Navigating the Nonprofit Landscape in the Digital Age

In today's rapidly evolving world, nonprofits' crucial role in addressing societal challenges and driving positive change has never been more crucial. As we navigate a landscape shaped by technological advancements, it is imperative for nonprofit organizations to adapt and innovate to effectively fulfill their missions.

The insights shared above underscore the importance of strategic planning, dedication, and leveraging innovative tools in the nonprofit sector. From the initial stages of establishing a nonprofit organization to navigating the complexities of compliance, engaging with stakeholders, and maximizing impact, each step requires careful consideration and proactive measures.

The guidance emphasizes the significance of seeking assistance from legal, accounting, and nonprofit professionals to ensure compliance with regulatory requirements. Moreover, integrating technology, such as artificial intelligence through ChatGPT, presents a valuable opportunity for nonprofits to enhance their operations, engage with their target audiences, and achieve their organizational goals more effectively.

Juliana Michael's exemplary leadership as the founder of two operational nonprofit organizations, America Thanking God, and

Christians in Technology, is a testament to the transformative potential of dedicated individuals driving meaningful change in their communities.

As we embark on this journey, let us remain steadfast in our commitment to making a positive impact, embracing innovation, and collaborating towards a brighter future for all.

Together, we can navigate the nonprofit landscape in the digital age with resilience, creativity, and a shared sense of purpose.

CHAPTER 1

INTRODUCTION TO

STARTING A NONPROFIT ORGANIZATION

In the diverse tapestry of societal fabric, nonprofit organizations stand as beacons of hope, catalysts of change, and guardians of compassion. With a steadfast commitment to addressing pressing issues, serving vulnerable populations, and fostering community well-being, nonprofits play a pivotal role in shaping a brighter, more equitable future for all. However, founding and incorporating a nonprofit organization is laden with complexities, challenges, and regulatory nuances, particularly in Georgia, as I use it as our primary guide. In this comprehensive guide, we embark on an in-depth exploration of the process of nonprofit incorporation in Georgia, offering step-by-step guidance, practical insights, and invaluable resources to empower aspiring founders in their mission-driven endeavors.

Understanding Nonprofit Incorporation
At its core, nonprofit incorporation formalizes an organization's commitment to its mission, governance structure, and legal standing. By incorporating as a nonprofit entity, organizations gain recognition as separate legal entities, distinct from their founders or members, with the ability to enter contracts, own

property, and pursue charitable activities. This chapter delves into the fundamental concepts of nonprofit incorporation, exploring its significance, benefits, and essential components.

Legal and Regulatory Framework in Georgia
Georgia's legal and regulatory framework governs the process of nonprofit incorporation, imposing specific requirements, procedures, and obligations on aspiring founders. From eligibility criteria to filing fees, governance structures, and compliance standards, understanding Georgia's nonprofit laws is essential for navigating the incorporation process effectively. This chapter provides a comprehensive overview of Georgia's legal and regulatory landscape, equipping founders with the knowledge and tools to ensure compliance and adherence to statutory requirements.

Preparing for Nonprofit Incorporation
Before embarking on the nonprofit incorporation journey, founders must thoroughly prepare, laying the groundwork for success. This chapter explores the preparatory steps of founding a nonprofit organization, from crafting mission and vision statements to developing governance documents, conducting research, and assembling a dedicated team of stakeholders. By investing time and effort in thoughtful preparation, founders can establish a strong foundation for their nonprofit's mission-driven work and organizational sustainability.

Step-by-Step Guide to Online Incorporation
In an increasingly digital age, the process of nonprofit incorporation has been streamlined through online platforms and electronic filing systems. This chapter offers a detailed, step-by-step guide to incorporating a nonprofit organization online in Georgia. From accessing the Georgia Secretary of State's website to completing the online application, paying filing fees, and obtaining confirmation of incorporation, aspiring founders are guided through each stage of the process with clarity and precision.

Post-Incorporation Obligations and Considerations

Beyond the act of incorporation, founders must navigate a myriad of post-incorporation obligations and considerations to ensure their nonprofit organizations' ongoing success and compliance. This chapter examines key post-incorporation tasks, including obtaining an Employer Identification Number (EIN), registering for state tax exemption, filing annual reports, maintaining financial records, and adhering to ethical governance standards. By proactively addressing post-incorporation requirements, founders can uphold transparency, accountability, and integrity in their nonprofit operations.

Resources and Support for Nonprofit Founders

Founders need help to walk the path to nonprofit incorporation. Resources, support networks, and educational opportunities exist to empower aspiring founders and enhance their capacity for success. This chapter highlights valuable resources available to nonprofit founders in Georgia, including online guides, legal clinics, training programs, and professional networks. By tapping into these resources and leveraging the expertise of industry professionals, founders can navigate the complexities of nonprofit incorporation with confidence and resilience.

Charting a Course for Nonprofit Excellence

As we conclude our exploration of nonprofit incorporation in Georgia, we reflect on the profound significance of mission-driven work, community engagement, and collective impact. Founding and incorporating a nonprofit organization is not merely a legal process but a transformative journey fueled by passion, purpose, and commitment to serving others. With dedication, perseverance, and a spirit of collaboration, aspiring founders in Georgia can chart a course for nonprofit excellence, realizing their vision of a more just, compassionate, and resilient society for generations to come.

In conclusion, the path to nonprofit incorporation is marked by challenges, opportunities, and the unwavering commitment of dedicated individuals. Through informed decision-making, strategic planning, and adherence to legal and regulatory standards, nonprofit founders can navigate this journey confidently and clearly, laying the groundwork for meaningful impact and enduring legacy in their communities and beyond.

Starting a nonprofit organization with 501(c)(3) status in the USA involves several steps. Here's a simplified guide:

Define Your Mission: Clearly articulate the purpose and goals of your organization. What issue or cause will you address?

Research and Planning: Research to ensure a need for your nonprofit in your community or field. Develop a business plan outlining your goals, strategies, budget, and target audience.

Choose a Name: Select a name for your nonprofit that reflects your mission and is unique. Check its availability and ensure it complies with state regulations.

Form a Board of Directors: Recruit individuals passionate about your cause and with diverse skills and expertise. The board will provide oversight and governance for your organization.

Incorporate Your Nonprofit: File articles of incorporation with your state's secretary of state office. Include your organization's name, purpose, address, and other required information.

Draft Bylaws: Create bylaws that outline your organization's internal rules and procedures, including board structure, decision-making processes, and membership criteria.

Apply for EIN: Obtain an Employer Identification Number (EIN) from the IRS. This unique identifier is necessary for tax purposes and banking.

File for 501(c) Status: Prepare and submit Form 1023 or Form 1023-EZ (for eligible organizations) to the IRS to apply for tax-exempt status. This process may involve providing detailed information about your organization's activities, finances, and governance structure.

Register with State Authorities: Depending on your state's regulations, you may need to register your nonprofit with state agencies for charitable solicitation, tax exemptions, and other purposes.

Develop Policies and Procedures: Create policies and procedures for financial management, fundraising, hiring practices, volunteer management, and other operational aspects of your organization.

Obtain Necessary Licenses and Permits: Research and secure any required licenses or permits to operate legally in your state or local jurisdiction.

Start Operations: Once you've received tax-exempt status and completed all necessary registrations, you can begin implementing your programs, fundraising, and serving your community.

Remember, starting a nonprofit requires time, dedication, and careful planning. Consider seeking assistance from legal, accounting, or nonprofit professionals to ensure compliance with all legal and regulatory requirements.

CHAPTER 2

Define Your Mission

Defining a nonprofit organization's mission-seeking 501(c) tax-exempt status is crucial in establishing its purpose and guiding its activities. The mission statement serves as the foundation upon which the organization is built, articulating its core values, goals, and intended impact on the community or causes it serves. Crafting a compelling and clear mission statement requires thoughtful consideration and alignment with the organization's vision and values. Here's a detailed guide on how to define your mission for your nonprofit 501(c) tax-exempt organization:

Introduction to Mission Definition:
Before delving into the specifics of crafting a mission statement, it's essential to understand the significance of this foundational element. The mission statement guides the organization, informing its strategic direction, decision-making processes, and day-to-day operations. It communicates the organization's purpose to stakeholders, including board members, staff, volunteers, donors, and the community. A well-defined mission statement inspires passion and commitment among stakeholders, attracts supporters, and enhances the organization's credibility and impact.

Key Components of a Mission Statement:

A strong mission statement typically contains several key components that collectively convey the essence of the organization's purpose and goals:

Vision: The aspirational future state that the organization seeks to achieve. It provides a compelling picture of the desired impact or outcome of the organization's work.

Purpose: The organization's purpose reflects the core values and beliefs that motivate its efforts. It answers the question, "Why does this organization exist, and what problem is it trying to solve?"

Target Population or Cause: The specific group of people, community, or issue the organization serves or addresses. This component clarifies the focus of the organization's activities and programs.

Values are the guiding principles and ethical standards that inform the organization's decision-making and behavior. Values reflect what is essential to the organization and how it operates.

Unique Approach or Differentiator: The distinctive methods, strategies, or approaches that set the organization apart from others in its field. This component highlights the organization's competitive advantage or unique contribution to addressing the identified need or problem.

Steps to Define Your Mission:

Crafting a mission statement involves systematic reflection, brainstorming, and refinement process. Follow these steps to define your nonprofit organization's mission:

Conduct Internal and External Assessment: Begin by conducting a thorough assessment of your organization's strengths, weaknesses, opportunities, and threats (SWOT analysis). Consider the external environment, including community needs, social trends, and competitor organizations. Identify any gaps or unmet needs your organization is uniquely positioned to address.

Engage Stakeholders: Involve key stakeholders, including board members, staff, volunteers, beneficiaries, and community members, in the mission definition process. Seek input, feedback, and perspectives from diverse voices to ensure that the mission statement reflects the collective vision and values of the organization.

Articulate Vision and Purpose: Clarify the desired future state (vision) your organization aims to achieve and the purpose or reason for its existence. Consider the broader societal or systemic change you aspire to contribute to and the specific outcomes or impact you seek to achieve.

Define Target Population or Cause: Identify the specific group of people, community, or issue your organization serves or addresses. Consider your target population's needs, challenges, and aspirations and how your organization can make a meaningful difference in their lives or communities.

Identify Core Values: Articulate the core values and ethical principles that guide your organization's actions, decisions, and relationships. These values should reflect the organization's identity, culture, and commitment to integrity, inclusivity, and accountability.

Highlight Unique Approach or Differentiator: Identify the distinctive methods, strategies, or approaches that set your organization apart from others in your field. Consider your organization's strengths, expertise, resources, and partnerships that enable you to deliver unique value and impact.

Draft Mission Statement: Based on the insights and inputs gathered through the previous steps, draft a mission statement that succinctly and effectively communicates the organization's vision, purpose, target population or cause, core values, and unique approach. Strive for clarity, brevity, and relevance, ensuring the mission statement resonates with stakeholders and inspires commitment and action.

Example Mission Statement:
Here's an example of a mission statement for a fictional nonprofit organization focused on providing education and empowerment

opportunities for underserved youth:

"Our mission is to empower underserved youth to reach their full potential through quality education, mentorship, and community engagement. Guided by our commitment to equity, inclusivity, and social justice, we provide innovative programs and resources that inspire lifelong learning, leadership, and positive social change. By partnering with schools, families, and community organizations, we create pathways to success and transform lives for a brighter future."

Conclusion:

Defining a nonprofit organization's mission is a foundational step in establishing its identity, purpose, and impact. By articulating a clear and compelling mission statement that reflects the organization's vision, values, and unique contributions, you can inspire stakeholders, attract support, and advance your mission with purpose and passion. Regularly revisit and refine your mission statement as your organization evolves and adapts to changing needs and opportunities, ensuring that it remains relevant, meaningful, and impactful in guiding your organization's journey toward positive social change.

CHAPTER 3

Research and Planning

Researching and planning for a nonprofit organization seeking 501(c) tax-exempt status is a critical process that lays the foundation for its success and impact. This comprehensive guide will outline the steps in conducting effective research and developing a strategic plan for your nonprofit organization.

Introduction:
Before diving into the specifics of research and planning, it's essential to understand the significance of this phase in the nonprofit startup process. Research and planning serve as the groundwork for building a sustainable and impactful organization by providing insights into your target community's needs, identifying potential challenges and opportunities, and developing strategies to achieve your mission effectively.

Identify Your Cause and Purpose:
The first step in planning for your nonprofit organization is clearly defining your cause and purpose. Reflect on the issues or challenges you are passionate about addressing and consider the impact you hope to achieve. Understand the scope and scale of the problem, the affected populations, and existing efforts to address

it. This will help you articulate a compelling mission statement that communicates your organization's purpose and focus.

Conduct Needs Assessment:
Once you've identified your cause and purpose, conduct a comprehensive needs assessment to understand better the needs and priorities of your target community or beneficiaries. This may involve analyzing demographic data, conducting surveys or interviews, and consulting with local organizations or experts in the field. Identify gaps or unmet needs that your organization can address and consider how your programs and services can best meet those needs.

Research Legal and Regulatory Requirements:
regulatory requirements governing nonprofit operations and tax-exempt status. Familiarize yourself with federal, state, and local laws and IRS regulations for obtaining 501(c) tax-exempt status. Determine the incorporation process, reporting requirements, and any licenses or permits required to operate legally in your jurisdiction.

Analyze the Competitive Landscape:
Research existing nonprofit organizations and initiatives working in your field or addressing similar issues. Identify potential collaborators, partners, and competitors to understand their approaches, strengths, and weaknesses. Analyze their programs, funding sources, and impact to identify opportunities for collaboration or differentiation. This research will inform your organization's positioning and strategy development.

Develop a Strategic Plan:
Based on your research findings, develop a strategic plan that outlines your organization's goals, objectives, and strategies for achieving its mission. A strategic plan provides a roadmap for your organization's growth and development, guiding decision-making, and resource allocation. Define your organization's vision, mission, values, and short-term and long-term goals. Identify target outcomes, performance indicators, and evaluation

methods to measure progress and impact.

Create a Budget and Financial Plan:
Develop a comprehensive budget and financial plan to support your organization's operations, programs, and growth initiatives. Estimate the costs associated with startup expenses, program development, staffing, fundraising, and overhead expenses. Identify potential funding sources, including grants, donations, and earned income, and develop strategies to diversify your revenue streams. Ensure your budget aligns with your organization's mission, goals, and financial sustainability.

Establish Governance Structure:
Define your organization's governance structure, including the roles and responsibilities of the board of directors, officers, and staff members. Develop bylaws that outline the organization's decision-making processes, voting procedures, and conflict-resolution mechanisms. Ensure that your governance structure promotes transparency, accountability, and effective leadership, aligning with best practices and legal requirements.

Develop Marketing and Communication Strategies:
Create marketing and communication strategies to raise awareness about your organization's mission, programs, and impact. Identify target audiences, key messages, and communication channels to reach stakeholders, including donors, volunteers, beneficiaries, and the community. Develop a branding strategy to effectively convey your organization's identity and values, including a logo, website, and marketing materials.

Implement Monitoring and Evaluation Systems:
Establish monitoring and evaluation systems to track progress, measure outcomes, and assess the effectiveness of your organization's programs and initiatives. Define performance indicators, data collection methods, and evaluation criteria to monitor programmatic impact and inform decision-making.

Collect feedback from stakeholders and continuously use evaluation findings to improve your organization's impact.

Review and Iterate:

Finally, regularly review and iterate on your organization's research and planning efforts to adapt to changing needs, trends, and opportunities. Monitor external factors, such as policy changes, funding trends, and community dynamics that may impact your organization's operations and strategies. Continuously seek stakeholder feedback and evaluate your organization's performance to ensure alignment with its mission and goals.

In conclusion, conducting thorough research and strategic planning is essential for the success and sustainability of a nonprofit organization seeking 501(c)(3) tax-exempt status. By identifying your cause, understanding community needs, complying with legal requirements, and developing a strategic plan, you can establish a strong foundation for your organization's mission-driven work. With careful planning and execution, your nonprofit can make a meaningful impact and contribute to positive social change.

CHAPTER 4

Choose a Name

Choosing a name for your nonprofit organization seeking 501(c) tax-exempt status is a significant decision that can impact its identity, branding, and recognition in the community. A well-chosen name should reflect your organization's mission and values, resonate with your target audience, and comply with legal requirements. This comprehensive guide will explore the key considerations and steps in selecting a name for your nonprofit organization.

Introduction:
Choosing a name for your nonprofit organization is more than just selecting words. It's about creating an identity that embodies your organization's mission, vision, and values. A carefully chosen name can inspire trust, convey professionalism, and attract supporters to your cause. In this guide, we'll discuss the importance of selecting the right name, explore creative brainstorming strategies, and provide practical tips for ensuring your chosen name is available and legally compliant.

Understand the Importance of Choosing the Right Name:
Before diving into the process of selecting a name, it's essential to understand why choosing the right name is crucial for your nonprofit organization:

Brand Identity: Your organization's name is a key component of

its brand identity, shaping how it is perceived by stakeholders, including donors, volunteers, and the community.
Recognition and Visibility: A memorable and distinctive name can help your organization stand out in a crowded marketplace and increase its visibility and recognition.
Mission Alignment: Your organization's name should reflect its mission and values, conveying a sense of purpose and commitment to its cause.
Legal Compliance: Choosing a legally compliant name ensures that your organization can operate smoothly and avoid potential conflicts or trademark issues.
Brainstorm Ideas:
Brainstorming is essential in choosing a name for your nonprofit organization. Here are some creative strategies to generate name ideas:
Mission and Values: Reflect on your organization's mission, values, and core beliefs. Consider words or phrases that capture the essence of your mission and convey the impact you hope to achieve.
Inspiration from Stories or Symbols: Draw inspiration from stories, symbols, or historical figures that are meaningful to your cause. Look for names that evoke emotions or convey a powerful message.
Wordplay and Creativity: Experiment with wordplay, alliteration, or creative word combinations to develop unique and memorable names. Consider using metaphors, imagery, or evocative language to capture attention.
Feedback and Collaboration: Involve stakeholders, including board members, staff, volunteers, and beneficiaries, in the brainstorming process. Encourage open dialogue and collaboration to generate diverse perspectives and ideas.

Consider Practical Factors:
In addition to creativity and alignment with your organization's mission, consider practical factors when choosing a name:
Memorability: Choose a name that is easy to remember and

pronounce. Avoid complex or obscure names that may be difficult for people to recall or spell.

Availability: Before finalizing a name, research its availability to ensure another organization still needs to use it. Check domain availability for a website and social media handles to secure your online presence.

Legal Compliance: Ensure your chosen name complies with legal requirements, including trademark laws and state regulations. Conduct a trademark search to verify that another entity does not already trademark your name.

Longevity: Choose a name that will remain relevant and meaningful over time. Consider how your organization's mission and scope may evolve and select a name that can adapt to changes.

Conduct Research and Due Diligence:

Once you've generated a list of potential name ideas, conduct thorough research and due diligence to assess their viability and availability:

Trademark Search: Conduct a trademark search to determine if your chosen name is available for use and not already trademarked by another organization. Search online databases, such as the United States Patent and Trademark Office (USPTO) database, to check for existing trademarks.

Business Entity Search: Check with your state's Secretary of State office to verify the availability of your chosen name for incorporation as a nonprofit organization. Ensure that another business entity still needs to register the name.

Domain Availability: To secure your organization's online presence, check the availability of domain names for your chosen name. Look for variations or alternative spellings if your preferred domain name is unavailable.

Test and Evaluate:

Once you've narrowed down your list of potential name ideas, test them with key stakeholders and evaluate their effectiveness:

Feedback Sessions: Organize feedback sessions with board members, staff, volunteers, and other stakeholders to gather input on the name options. Ask for feedback on each name's clarity, relevance, and appeal.

Survey or Poll: Conduct a survey or poll among your target audience to gather broader feedback on the name options. Use online survey tools or social media platforms to reach a wider audience and collect responses.

Focus Groups: Consider organizing focus groups to conduct in-depth discussions and qualitative analysis of the name options. Gather insights into how different names are perceived and which resonate most strongly with participants.

Finalize and Register Your Name:

Once you've selected a name for your nonprofit organization, take the following steps to finalize and
register it:

Incorporation: Register your chosen name with your state's Secretary of State office as part of your nonprofit organization's incorporation process. Follow the procedures and submit the necessary paperwork to establish your organization officially.

Trademark Registration: Consider registering your organization's name as a trademark to protect its exclusive use and prevent others from using it without permission. Consult a trademark attorney to guide you through the registration process and ensure legal protection.

Domain Registration: Secure the domain name for your organization's website to establish an online presence and enhance its visibility. Register the domain name through a reputable domain registrar and consider purchasing variations or alternative extensions to protect your brand.

Social Media Handles: Claim your organization's name on social media platforms to reserve your brand identity and prevent others from using it. Use your chosen name to create profiles on relevant platforms, such as Facebook, Twitter, Instagram, and LinkedIn.

Choosing a name for your nonprofit organization is a significant decision that requires careful consideration, creativity, and research. Following the steps outlined in this guide, you can select a name that reflects your organization's mission and values, resonates with your target audience, and complies with legal requirements. A well-chosen name can be a powerful tool for building brand identity, increasing visibility, and advancing your organization's mission and impact. With thoughtful planning and collaboration, you can choose a name that embodies the essence of your organization and inspires others to join you in making a difference.

CHAPTER 5

Form a Board of Directors

Forming a Board of Directors is a critical step in establishing a nonprofit organization seeking 501(c) tax-exempt status in the United States. The Board plays a crucial role in providing governance, oversight, and strategic direction to the organization, ensuring its mission is fulfilled effectively and responsibly. This comprehensive guide will explore forming a Board of Directors for your nonprofit organization, including key roles and responsibilities, recruitment strategies, and best practices for building a diverse and effective board.

Introduction:

The Board of Directors serves as the governing body of a nonprofit organization and is responsible for setting its strategic direction, overseeing its operations, and ensuring accountability to stakeholders. Forming a Board of Directors is a critical step in the startup process for a nonprofit seeking 501(c) tax-exempt status, as it provides essential leadership and guidance to the organization. In this guide, we will outline the steps involved in forming a Board of Directors, including defining roles and responsibilities, recruiting board members, and establishing effective governance practices.

Define Roles and Responsibilities:

Before recruiting board members, it's essential to define the roles and responsibilities of the Board of Directors and clarify the expectations for board members. Key responsibilities of the Board typically include:

Providing strategic direction and long-term planning for the organization.

Overseeing the organization's financial management and ensuring fiscal responsibility.

Monitoring organizational performance and evaluating progress toward goals.

Hiring, supporting, and evaluating the executive director or CEO.

Ensuring compliance with legal and regulatory requirements, including maintaining 501(c) tax-exempt status.

Representing the interests of stakeholders, including donors, beneficiaries, and the community.

Fundraising and resource development to support the organization's mission and programs.

By clearly defining the Board's roles and responsibilities, you can attract board members who are committed to fulfilling their duties and contributing to the organization's success.

Identify Desired Skills and Expertise:

When recruiting board members, it's crucial to identify the desired skills, expertise, and diversity needed to support the organization's mission and strategic priorities. Consider the following factors when defining the desired composition of the Board:

Include expertise in relevant fields, such as finance, law, marketing, fundraising, or programmatic areas related to the organization's mission.

Experience serving on nonprofit boards or volunteering in leadership roles.

Diversity in terms of backgrounds, perspectives, and lived experiences to ensure inclusive decision-making and representation of the community served by the organization.

Networks and connections that can help the organization access resources, partnerships, and opportunities for collaboration.

Commitment to the organization's mission and values, including a willingness to advocate for its interests and support its fundraising efforts.

By identifying the desired skills and expertise needed on the Board, you can target your recruitment efforts to attract individuals who can contribute effectively to the organization's success.

Recruit Board Members:

Recruiting board members is a strategic process that involves identifying potential candidates, assessing their qualifications, and inviting them to join the Board. Here are some strategies for recruiting board members:

Network within your community: Reach out to your personal and professional networks to identify individuals interested in serving on the Board. Attend networking events, community meetings, and professional conferences to connect with potential candidates.

Engage current stakeholders: Involve current staff members, volunteers, donors, and beneficiaries in the recruitment process by soliciting their recommendations and referrals. They may know individuals passionate about the organization's mission and willing to serve on the Board.

Use online platforms: Utilize online platforms, such as LinkedIn, BoardMatch, or nonprofit job boards, to advertise board openings and attract candidates with the desired skills and expertise. Create a clear and compelling recruitment message outlining the organization's mission, expectations for board members, and the benefits of serving on the Board.

Orient and Onboard Board Members:

Once you've recruited board members, providing them with the information and support they need to fulfill their roles effectively is essential. Develop an orientation and onboarding process to familiarize new board members with the organization's mission, programs, policies, and procedures. This may include:

Ensure you provide an orientation packet or handbook with

essential information about the organization's history, mission statement, bylaws, strategic plan, board structure, and key contacts.

Schedule one-on-one meetings with board leadership, staff members, and key stakeholders to introduce new board members to the organization's culture, values, and operations.

Facilitate board orientation sessions or retreats to engage new members in strategic planning, goal setting, and team-building activities.

Assign mentors or buddy board members to support new members during their transition onto the Board and provide ongoing guidance and support.

Investing in a robust orientation and onboarding process can set new board members up for success and ensure a smooth transition into their roles.

Establish Effective Governance Practices:

You must ensure the effectiveness and accountability of the Board of Directors; it's crucial to establish and adhere to best practices in governance. Consider implementing the following practices to promote transparency, integrity, and responsible stewardship:

Regular board meetings: Schedule meetings to review organizational performance, discuss strategic priorities, and decide on crucial issues. Establish a meeting schedule and agenda in advance and promptly distribute materials and reports to board members.

Form committees or working groups to address specific areas of governance, such as finance, fundraising, governance, and program oversight. Assign clear roles and responsibilities to committee members and provide them with the support and resources needed to fulfill their mandates.

Financial oversight: Establish financial controls and policies to ensure the organization's fiscal responsibility and integrity. Develop an annual budget, review financial reports regularly, and conduct audits or reviews as necessary to monitor compliance with financial policies and regulatory requirements.

Board evaluation: Conduct periodic evaluations of the Board's performance to assess its effectiveness, identify areas for improvement, and enhance its governance practices. Solicit feedback from board members, staff, and stakeholders through surveys, interviews, or facilitated discussions, and use the findings to inform board development and training efforts.

Conflict of interest policy: Adopt a conflict-of-interest policy to address and manage conflicts of interest among board members, staff, volunteers, or other stakeholders. Board members must disclose any potential conflicts of interest and abstain from participating in decisions where they have a personal or financial interest.

Legal compliance: Ensure that the organization complies with all legal and regulatory requirements governing nonprofit organizations, including maintaining 501(c) tax-exempt status, filing required reports and filings with government agencies, and adhering to relevant laws and regulations.

By establishing effective governance practices, you can promote accountability, transparency, and ethical conduct within the organization, enhancing its credibility and trustworthiness with stakeholders.

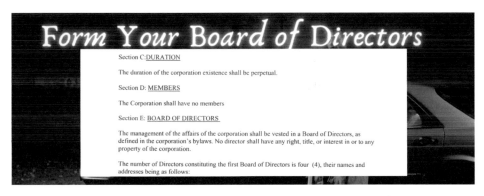

In Conclusion, forming a Board of Directors is a foundational step in establishing a nonprofit organization seeking 501(c)(3) tax-exempt status. By defining roles and responsibilities, recruiting qualified board members, and establishing effective governance practices, you can.

CHAPTER 6

Incorporate Your Nonprofit

Incorporating your nonprofit organization is crucial in obtaining 501(c) tax-exempt status in the United States. Incorporation provides legal recognition and protection for your organization, establishes its governance structure, and enables it to operate as a separate legal entity. This comprehensive guide will explore the steps in incorporating your nonprofit organization, including legal requirements, documentation, and best practices for ensuring compliance and effectiveness.

Introduction:
Incorporating your nonprofit organization is legally establishing it as a separate entity from its founders, providing it with limited liability and enabling it to enter contracts, own property, and pursue its mission independently. By incorporating, your organization gains legal recognition and protection, enhances its credibility and accountability, and lays the foundation for obtaining 501(c)(3) tax-exempt status from the Internal Revenue Service (IRS). This guide will outline the steps in incorporating your nonprofit organization and provide practical tips for navigating the process effectively.

Understand Legal Requirements:
Before initiating the incorporation process, it's essential to understand the legal requirements and obligations governing

nonprofit organizations in your state. While the specific requirements may vary depending on your state of incorporation, there are several key considerations to keep in mind:

State Laws: Research the nonprofit corporation laws in your state to understand the requirements for incorporating a nonprofit organization. Familiarize yourself with the applicable statutes, regulations, and filing procedures governing nonprofit corporations.

Articles of Incorporation: Prepare and file articles of incorporation with the appropriate state agency, typically the Secretary of State's office. The articles of incorporation outline essential information about your organization, including its name, purpose, duration, registered agent, and initial board of directors.

Bylaws: Develop bylaws for your organization, which are the internal rules and procedures governing its operations and governance structure. Include provisions related to board composition, decision-making processes, meetings, and officer roles and responsibilities.

Registered Agent: Designate a registered agent to serve as the organization's official point of contact for legal notices and service of process. The registered agent must have a physical address in the state where the organization is incorporated and be available during regular business hours.

Filing Fees: Pay any required filing fees for incorporating your nonprofit organization. The filing fees vary depending on your state of incorporation and may range from a nominal amount to several hundred dollars.

By understanding the legal requirements and obligations associated with incorporating your nonprofit organization, you can ensure compliance with state laws and streamline the incorporation process.

Choose a Name:

Selecting a name for your nonprofit organization is essential in the incorporation process. Your organization's name should reflect its mission, values, and identity and comply with state regulations governing corporate names. Consider the following guidelines when choosing a name:

Availability: Ensure that your chosen name is not already being used by another organization in your state. Check the Secretary of State's business entity database or conduct a name availability search to verify that your desired name is available for use.

Legal Compliance: Comply with state regulations governing corporate names, including restrictions on certain words or phrases and requirements for designations such as "Corporation," "Incorporated," or "Company."

Mission Alignment: Choose a name that accurately reflects your organization's mission, values, and purpose. Consider words or phrases that convey the impact you hope to achieve and resonate with your target audience.

Trademark Considerations: When choosing your organization's name, consider trademark considerations to avoid potential conflicts with existing trademarks. Conduct a trademark search to ensure that another entity still needs to trademark your chosen name.

By carefully selecting a name for your nonprofit organization, you can establish its identity and brand while ensuring compliance with legal requirements and avoiding potential conflicts.

Draft and File Articles of Incorporation:

Once you've chosen a name for your nonprofit organization, the next step is to prepare and file articles of incorporation with the appropriate state agency. The articles of incorporation are the legal documents that formally establish your organization as a nonprofit corporation and provide essential information about its structure and purpose. Here's an overview of the process:

Prepare Articles of Incorporation: Draft articles of incorporation for your nonprofit organization, including the required information such as the organization's name, purpose, duration, registered agent, and initial board of directors. You may use a template provided by your state's Secretary of State office or seek assistance from legal counsel to ensure compliance with state laws.

File Articles of Incorporation: Submit the articles of incorporation to the Secretary of State's office or the appropriate state agency responsible for processing corporate filings. Include any required filing fees with your submission and follow the specified filing procedures outlined by the state agency.

Obtain Certificate of Incorporation: Upon reviewing and approving your articles of incorporation, the state agency will issue a certificate of incorporation or similar document officially recognizing your nonprofit organization as a legal entity. Please keep a copy of the certificate for your records and use it to demonstrate your organization's legal status.

By drafting and filing articles of incorporation, you officially establish your nonprofit organization as a separate legal entity, providing it with limited liability and legal recognition under state law.

Develop Bylaws:

With the articles of incorporation filed, the next step is to develop bylaws for your nonprofit organization. Bylaws serve as the internal rules and procedures governing the operation and management of the organization, including its governance structure, decision-making processes, and officer roles and responsibilities. Here's how to develop bylaws for your nonprofit organization:

Outline Governance Structure: Define your organization's governance structure, including the composition of the board of directors, officer positions, and committee roles. Specify the responsibilities and authority of each governance body and establish procedures for elections, appointments, and terms of office.

Detail Meeting Procedures: Establish procedures for conducting board meetings, including the frequency of meetings, notice requirements, quorum, voting procedures, and record-keeping practices. Ensure that your bylaws comply with any legal requirements or regulations governing nonprofit corporations in your state.

Address Key Operational Issues: Address key operational issues in your bylaws, such as financial management, conflicts of interest, indemnification of directors and officers, and amendment procedures. Include provisions to safeguard the organization's assets, promote transparency and accountability, and mitigate potential risks.

Review and Approval: Review the draft bylaws with your board of directors and seek their input and feedback. Based on their feedback, make any necessary revisions or amendments, and ensure that the bylaws accurately reflect the organization's governance structure and operational procedures.

Adoption: Adopt the bylaws through a formal vote by the board of directors. Once adopted, distribute copies of the bylaws to all board members and officers and ensure they know their rights and responsibilities.

By developing bylaws for your nonprofit organization, you establish clear guidelines and procedures for governance and operations, promoting transparency, accountability, and effective decision-making.

Appoint Initial Board of Directors:

With the articles of incorporation filed and bylaws adopted, the next step is to appoint the initial board of directors for your nonprofit organization. The board of directors plays a crucial role in providing governance, oversight, and strategic direction to the organization, ensuring its mission is fulfilled effectively and responsibly. Here's how to appoint the initial board of directors:

Identify Candidates: Identify individuals who are willing and qualified to serve on the board of directors of your nonprofit organization. Consider their expertise and experience.

STATE OF GEORGIA REGISTERING PROCESS AS A CASE STUDY

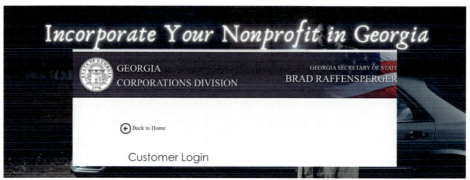

Registering with state authorities for your 501(c) tax-exempt certificate in Atlanta, Georgia, involves several steps, especially if your nonprofit deals with specific activities like food handling or public gatherings. Here's a step-by-step guide tailored to such scenarios:

Determine Licensing and Permit Requirements:

If your nonprofit deals with food, you must obtain a food service license from the Georgia Department of Public Health. Determine the specific requirements for obtaining this license based on your organization's food-related activities, such as food preparation, distribution, or catering.

Contact the Georgia Department of Public Health:

Contact the Georgia Department of Public Health for the necessary licenses and permits for your organization's food-related activities. They can provide guidance on the application process, required documentation, and any training or certification requirements.

Complete Required Training or Certification Courses:

Depending on the nature of your organization's food-related activities, you may need to complete training or certification courses in food safety and handling. The Georgia Department of Public Health or local health departments often offer these courses covering foodborne illness prevention, sanitation practices, and proper food handling techniques.

Apply for Food Service License:
Once you've completed any required training or certification courses and gathered the necessary documentation, apply for a food service license from the Georgia Department of Public Health. Provide all requested information, pay applicable fees, and undergo any required inspections or evaluations of your facilities.

Obtain Other Necessary Permits or Certificates:
Your organization may need other permits or certificates and a food service license, depending on its specific activities. For example, if you plan to host public gatherings or events, you may need temporary food service, event, or alcohol permits. Research the requirements for these permits and obtain them as needed from the appropriate authorities.

Maintain Compliance and Renewals:
Once your organization has obtained the necessary licenses, permits, and certificates, it's essential to maintain compliance with all applicable regulations and requirements. This includes adhering to food safety guidelines, renewing licenses and permits as needed, and staying up to date on changes in state or local regulations.

Consider Liability Insurance:
Depending on the nature of your organization's activities, consider obtaining liability insurance to protect against potential risks and liabilities associated with food service or public gatherings. Consult with an insurance provider specializing in nonprofit organizations to explore options and determine the coverage best suits your needs.

By following these steps and staying informed about state and local regulations, your nonprofit organization can register with state authorities for its 501(c)(3) tax-exempt certificate in Atlanta, Georgia, while ensuring compliance with licensing and permit requirements related to food handling and public gatherings.

Step 1: Visit the Georgia Secretary of State's Website
Go to the Georgia Secretary of State's website: Georgia Secretary of State.
Navigate to the "Corporations" section.
Step : Access the Online Filing System
Look for the option to "Incorporate a Business" or "Register a corporation" and click on it.
You may need to create an account or log in if you already have one.
Step 3: Complete the Online Application
Follow the prompts to fill out the online application for nonprofit incorporation.
Please provide information about your nonprofit, including its name, purpose, registered agent, and governing documents (articles of incorporation).
Double-check all information for accuracy before proceeding.
Step 4: Pay the Filing Fee
Once you've completed the application, you'll be prompted to pay the filing fee.
As of the date of this writing, the filing fee for nonprofit incorporation in Georgia is $100.
Follow the instructions to secure online payment using a credit or debit card.
Step 5: Submit the Application
After payment is processed, review the application one final time to ensure everything is correct.
Apply electronically through the online filing system.
Step 6: Obtain Confirmation
Once your application is submitted, you should receive a confirmation email or notification.
This confirmation proves that your nonprofit's incorporation application has been successfully filed with the Georgia Secretary of State.
Step 7: Obtain an EIN

After receiving confirmation of your nonprofit's incorporation, apply for an Employer Identification Number (EIN) from the Internal Revenue Service (IRS) website.

This number is necessary for tax purposes and can be obtained free of charge.

Step 8: Additional Steps

Depending on your nonprofit's activities and plans, you may need to take additional steps such as registering for state tax exemption, applying for charitable solicitation registration, or filing other necessary forms with state agencies.

You can successfully incorporate your nonprofit organization in Georgia by following these steps and completing the online application through the Georgia Secretary of State's website.

How to Incorporate Your Nonprofit in Georgia

Step 1: Open your preferred web browser and navigate to https://ecorp.sos.ga.gov/.

Step 2: If you're a new user, create an account by selecting the option to register. Choose a username and password to set up your account.

Step 3: Once logged in, click "Online Services" to access the online filing system.

Step 4: Select "Create or Register a Business from the menu options," which is typically displayed as one of the wine-colored boxes. Then, choose "I am creating a new domestic business" to proceed.

Step 5: Select your business type and subtype from the dropdown list provided. You may also upload any supporting documents, though this step is optional.

Step 6: Enter your preferred business name as agreed upon with your board of directors. When prompted, select "No" if you do not have a business name reservation number or name.

Step 7: Fill in all required information, including your principal office address, registered agent details, member information, and incorporator details.

Step 8: As the incorporator, enter your name as the authorized signature.

Step 9: Review all entered information for accuracy, then click the "Submit" button to proceed to the payment step.

Step 10: Enter your payment details to complete the filing process. The filing fee for incorporating a nonprofit in Georgia is $100.

How to Professionally Handle a Revoked 501(c)(3) Status

Receiving IRS Notice CP120A Notice of Revocation of Tax-Exempt Status is challenging for any nonprofit organization. The IRS automatically revokes the 501(c)(3) tax-exempt status of nonprofits that fail to file Form 990 for three consecutive years without prior warning or the possibility of appeal. Fortunately, the IRS provides a process for reinstating 501(c)(3) status. This guide outlines the professional steps your nonprofit should take if it faces this situation.

Step 1: Publicly Address Your 501(c)(3) Status Revocation

Upon revocation, your nonprofit is no longer recognized as a tax-exempt charity, meaning donations to your organization are not tax-deductible. It is crucial to update all channels that mention your 501(c)(3) status to reflect this change.

Donation Solicitations: Remove any language suggesting that donations are tax-deductible.

Organization's Website: Update any descriptions that label your nonprofit as a "tax-exempt organization." Consider adding a brief notice explaining the revocation and outlining your next steps.

Communication Channels: Review and revise email templates, social media profiles, and newsletters to remove references to your 501(c)(3) status.

Transparency is key. Misleading donors about your tax-exempt status can lead to legal consequences and erode trust. Clear communication helps maintain donor confidence and demonstrates your commitment to transparency.

Step 2: Do Not File New Articles of Incorporation

Your nonprofit's state incorporation remains valid despite revoking your 501(c)(3) status. This status establishes your nonprofit as a legal entity, separate from its federal tax designation. Verify that your corporate status is active with your state by ensuring all state requirements, such as filing corporate annual reports, are current. There is no need to file new Articles of Incorporation.

Step 3: Apply for 501(c)(3) Status Reinstatement

To regain your tax-exempt status, you must reapply to the IRS using Form 1023, indicating that it is an application for reinstatement. Provide detailed information about your past activities and file any missing Form 990s based on your nonprofit's financial history:

Form 990-N: For organizations with annual gross receipts of $50,000 or less. If you missed three years of this form, you do not need to file the missed years with your reinstatement application.

Form 990-EZ: For organizations with annual gross receipts under $200,000 and total assets under $500,000. If this form was required in any missed years, prepare and file it with your application.

Form 990 (Standard Form): For organizations with annual gross receipts over $200,000 and total assets over $500,000. Prepare and file this form for all three years if required.

Form 990-PF: For private foundations, regardless of financial status.

Be prepared for follow-up questions from the IRS if your application demonstrates continued compliance with 501(c)(3) requirements, your tax-exempt status should be restored.

Step 4: Prevent Future Revocations

To avoid future revocations, maintain compliance with all IRS requirements. File Form 990 annually and keep complete and accurate financial records. Regularly updating these records is not just best practice but a legal requirement.

If maintaining internal compliance is challenging, consider outsourcing to professionals. Ensuring your nonprofit meets all regulatory obligations.

Maintaining Your 501(c)(3) Status

Consistent compliance and transparency are crucial to maintaining your nonprofit's 501(c)(3) status. By filing Form 990 annually and keeping thorough records, you safeguard your organization's tax-exempt status and build trust with donors and stakeholders.

If your nonprofit has received Notice CP120A, there is still time to act. Professional services can assist with the reinstatement process, ensuring your organization regains its tax-exempt status smoothly.

Conclusion

Establishing and maintaining a 501(c)(3) tax-exempt status is vital for nonprofit organizations. It not only provides financial benefits but also enhances credibility and trust. Addressing a revocation professionally without filing new Articles of Incorporation, applying for reinstatement correctly, and preventing future issues through diligent compliance ensures your nonprofit continues to operate effectively and maintains the support of its community and donors. Following these steps, you can navigate the challenges of a revoked 501(c)(3) status and emerge with a more vital, resilient organization.

CHAPTER 7

Drafting and Writing a Perfect Bylaws

Drafting and writing bylaws for your nonprofit organization is crucial in establishing its governance structure and operational procedures. Bylaws serve as the internal rules and regulations that govern how your organization operates, including the roles and responsibilities of board members, decision-making processes, meeting procedures, and other key operational matters. Creating well-crafted bylaws ensures transparency, accountability, and compliance with legal requirements, particularly for nonprofits seeking 501(c) tax-exempt status. In this comprehensive guide, we will explore the process of drafting and writing perfect bylaws for your nonprofit organization, covering key components, best practices, and examples to help you create effective governing documents.

Introduction:

Bylaws are the backbone of any nonprofit organization, providing the framework for its governance and operations. Drafting and writing perfect bylaws for your nonprofit organization is a critical task that requires careful consideration and attention to detail. Well-crafted bylaws serve as a roadmap for the organization's leadership, guiding decision-making processes, ensuring accountability, and promoting transparency. In this guide, we will walk through the process of drafting and writing bylaws for your nonprofit organization, covering key components, best practices, and examples to help you create effective governing documents.

Understand the Purpose and Importance of Bylaws:

Before diving into drafting bylaws, it's essential to understand the purpose and importance of these governing documents. Bylaws serve several critical functions within a nonprofit organization:

Establish Governance Structure: Bylaws outline the organization's governance structure, including the composition of the board of directors, officer positions, and committee roles.

Define Operational Procedures: Bylaws establish procedures for conducting meetings, making decisions, and managing day-to-day operations, ensuring consistency and efficiency in the organization's activities.

Clarify Rights and Responsibilities: Bylaws define the rights and responsibilities of board members, officers, and other stakeholders, providing clarity and guidance on their roles within the organization.

Ensure Compliance: Bylaws ensure compliance with legal and regulatory requirements governing nonprofit organizations, including state laws, IRS regulations, and best practices in governance and management.

Promote Transparency and Accountability: Bylaws promote transparency and accountability by outlining procedures for financial management, conflict resolution, and decision-making and establishing mechanisms for oversight and reporting.

Understanding the purpose and importance of bylaws is essential for creating effective governing documents that support a nonprofit organization's mission and objectives.

Determine Key Components of Bylaws:

Before drafting your bylaws, it's important to determine the key components and provisions that should be included in the document. While the specific contents of bylaws may vary depending on the organization's size, structure, and mission, there are several essential components that should be addressed:

Name and Purpose: Begin by stating the organization's name and primary purpose or mission. This section should provide a clear and concise statement of the organization's goals and objectives.

Membership: If your organization has members, specify the qualifications for membership, rights and responsibilities of members, and procedures for admitting, suspending, or terminating membership.

Board of Directors: Outline the composition of the board of directors, including the number of directors, qualifications, terms of office, and procedures for electing or appointing directors. Define the powers, duties, and responsibilities of the board, including oversight of the organization's activities and decision-making authority.

Officers: Identify the officer positions within the organization, such as president, vice president, treasurer, and secretary. Specify the duties and responsibilities of each officer, as well as the process for electing or appointing officers and filling vacancies.

Meetings: Establish procedures for conducting board meetings, including notice requirements, quorum, voting procedures, and record-keeping practices. Define the frequency and format of meetings, as well as any special or emergency meeting provisions.

Committees: If your organization has committees, outline their composition, powers, and duties. Specify the process for appointing committee members, selecting committee chairs, and reporting to the board.

Financial Management: Establish procedures for financial management, including budgeting, accounting, and reporting. Define the authority to handle financial transactions, sign checks, and access bank accounts, and specify any requirements for financial oversight and audits.

Amendments: Include provisions for amending the bylaws, specifying the process for proposing, adopting, and implementing changes. Define the voting requirements and procedures for amending the bylaws, ensuring that any amendments are made in accordance with legal requirements and organizational policies.

By determining the key components of your bylaws, you can create a comprehensive and effective governing document that addresses the needs and priorities of your nonprofit organization.

Research Applicable Laws and Regulations:
Before drafting your bylaws, research applicable laws, regulations, and best practices governing nonprofit organizations in your state and at the federal level. Familiarize yourself with state nonprofit corporation laws, IRS regulations for tax-exempt organizations, and any other relevant statutes or regulations that may impact your organization's governance and operations. Consider consulting legal counsel or nonprofit experts to ensure that your bylaws comply with legal requirements and industry standards. Pay special attention to any specific provisions or requirements for nonprofits seeking 501(c) tax-exempt status, such as restrictions on lobbying and political activities, public disclosure requirements, and rules for maintaining tax-exempt status.

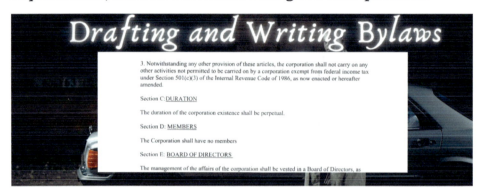

Draft Bylaws:
Once you've determined the key components and researched applicable laws and regulations, it's time to draft your bylaws. Start by outlining each section and provision based on the key elements identified earlier, ensuring clarity, consistency, and completeness. Use clear and concise language, avoiding jargon or technical terminology that may be unclear to readers. Consider including examples, explanations, or annotations to clarify complex provisions or legal concepts. As you draft your bylaws, keep the following best practices in mind:
Be Specific and Detailed: Provide clear and detailed instructions for each section and provision of the bylaws, leaving no room for

ambiguity or interpretation. Clearly define.

CHAPTER 8

Apply for EIN

Applying for an Employer Identification Number (EIN) is a crucial step for any nonprofit organization, especially those seeking 501(c) tax-exempt status in the United States. An EIN serves as the unique identifier for your organization, allowing you to open bank accounts, apply for tax-exempt status, hire employees, and engage in various financial transactions. In this comprehensive guide, we will explore the process of applying for an EIN for your nonprofit organization, covering key steps, requirements, and best practices to ensure a smooth and successful application.

Introduction:
Obtaining an Employer Identification Number (EIN) is an essential administrative task for any nonprofit organization operating in the United States. An EIN serves as the organization's tax identification number, allowing it to conduct various financial transactions, including opening bank accounts, applying for tax-exempt status, and filing tax returns. For nonprofit organizations seeking 501(c) tax-exempt status, obtaining an EIN is a prerequisite for applying for tax-exempt status from the Internal Revenue Service (IRS). In this guide, we will walk through the process of applying for an EIN for your nonprofit organization, covering key steps, requirements, and best practices to ensure a successful application.

Understand the Purpose of an EIN:

Before applying for an EIN, it's essential to understand the purpose and significance of this unique identifier. An EIN, or a Federal Tax Identification Number, is a nine-digit number the IRS assigns to identify your organization for tax purposes. Some key functions of an EIN for nonprofit organizations include:

Tax Reporting: An EIN reports income, assets, and expenses on tax returns filed with the IRS, including Form 990 for tax-exempt organizations.

Employment Taxes: If your nonprofit organization has employees, an EIN is required for reporting and remitting payroll taxes, including federal income tax withholding, Social Security, and Medicare taxes.

Banking and Financial Transactions: An EIN is necessary for opening bank accounts, applying for loans or lines of credit, and engaging in other financial transactions on behalf of the organization.

Tax-Exempt Status: For nonprofit organizations seeking 501(c) tax-exempt status, an EIN is required as part of the application process with the IRS.

Understanding the purpose and importance of an EIN will help you navigate the application process and ensure compliance with tax and regulatory requirements.

Determine Eligibility for an EIN:

Most nonprofit organizations, including those seeking 501(c) tax-exempt status, can apply for an EIN. However, there are specific requirements and restrictions to be aware of:

Legal Structure: Your organization must be organized as a corporation, trust, estate, or other legal entity recognized under state law to qualify for an EIN. Unincorporated associations, such as informal community groups or clubs, may not be eligible.

Tax-Exempt Status: While obtaining tax-exempt status is not a prerequisite for applying for an EIN, organizations seeking 501(c) tax-exempt status must obtain an EIN as part of the application process with the IRS.

Sole Proprietorships: If you operate as a sole proprietorship with no employees, you may use your Social Security Number (SSN) instead of an EIN for tax reporting purposes. However, obtaining an EIN is still recommended to separate your personal and business finances.

Before applying for an EIN, verify that your organization meets the eligibility requirements and has the necessary documentation and information ready for application.

Gather Required Information:

Before applying for an EIN, gather the required information and documentation to complete the application accurately. Key information and documents you'll need include:

Legal Name of Organization: Provide the full legal name of your nonprofit organization as it appears on official documents, including articles of incorporation or formation.

Taxpayer Identification Number (TIN): If applicable, provide the taxpayer identification number (TIN) of any individuals or entities associated with the organization, such as trustees, officers, or owners.

Legal Structure: Indicate your organization's legal structure, such as a corporation, trust, estate, or other entity type recognized under state law.

Reason for Applying: Specify the reason for applying for an EIN, such as starting a new business, hiring employees, or applying for tax-exempt status.

Principal Officer: Provide the name, title, and Social Security Number (SSN) or individual taxpayer identification number (ITIN) of the organization's principal officer or responsible party.

Business Address: Provide the organization's physical address, including the street address, city, state, and ZIP code. This address will be used as the organization's principal place of business.

Contact Information: Provide contact information for the organization, including a phone number and email address where the IRS can reach you if additional information is needed.

Gathering all required information and documentation in

advance will streamline the application process and help ensure that your application is accurate and complete.

To register for an Employer Identification Number (EIN) under the jurisdiction of the Atlanta, Georgia, IRS office, you can apply online through the IRS website. Here are the steps to apply online for an EIN:

Step 1: Access the IRS Website:
Navigate to the Internal Revenue Service (IRS) official website at www.irs.gov.

Step 2: Find the EIN Application Page:
Locate the "Employer Identification Number (EIN)" page on the IRS website. You can typically find this by searching for "EIN" in the search bar or navigating through the "Forms & Instructions" section.

Step 3: Choose the Online Application Option:
Select the option to apply for an EIN online. The IRS offers an online application process called "Apply for an Employer Identification Number (EIN) Online."

Step 4: Begin the Application:
Click on the link or button to start the online EIN application process. You will be directed to the online application form.

Step 5: Provide Required Information:
Enter all required information accurately into the online application form. This includes details about your nonprofit organization, such as its legal name, address, legal structure, and reason for applying.

Step 6: Principal Officer Information:
Provide the name, title, and Social Security Number (SSN) or Individual Taxpayer Identification Number (ITIN) of the organization's principal officer or responsible party. This individual will be designated the "responsible party" for the EIN application.

Step 7: Review and Confirm Information:
Carefully review all the information you entered before applying.

Ensure that all details are accurate and up to date.
Step 8: Submit the Application:
Once you have reviewed and confirmed the information, submit the online application. You may receive an immediate notification of your EIN assignment upon successful submission.
Step 9: Save Confirmation Document:
After applying, save or print the confirmation document for your records. This document will include your newly assigned EIN, which you will need for various tax and administrative purposes.
Step 10: Use Your EIN:
Once you receive your EIN, you can use it for various purposes, such as opening bank accounts, applying for tax-exempt status, and filing tax returns.
Following these steps and applying online through the IRS website, you can obtain an Employer Identification Number (EIN) for your nonprofit organization registered under the Atlanta, Georgia, IRS office jurisdiction.

Please Note:
The fee to apply for an Employer Identification Number (EIN) from the Internal Revenue Service (IRS) is $0 (zero dollars). The IRS does not charge a fee for applying for an EIN online or by mail. The application process is free of charge, regardless of whether you are applying for a new EIN, requesting a replacement EIN, or updating the information associated with an existing EIN.

It's important to note that while the IRS does not charge a fee for the EIN application itself, there may be fees associated with other services or processes related to your nonprofit organization, such as filing certain tax forms, obtaining tax-exempt status, or requesting additional services from the IRS or third-party providers.

When applying for an EIN online through the IRS website, you do not need to provide any payment information or submit payment for the application. Follow the steps outlined in the online application process, provide the required information, and apply electronically. Once your application is processed and approved, you will receive your free EIN.

CHAPTER 9

File for 501(c)Status!

Applying for 501(c) tax-exempt status is a significant milestone for nonprofit organizations in the United States. Obtaining this designation allows nonprofits to be exempt from federal income tax and receive tax-deductible donations. However, the process of applying for 501(c) status can be complex and time-consuming, requiring careful preparation and adherence to IRS guidelines. This comprehensive guide will walk through the steps in applying for your nonprofit organization's 501(c) status, covering key requirements, best practices, and tips to ensure a successful application.

Introduction:
Securing 501(c) tax-exempt status is a critical step for nonprofit organizations seeking to achieve their missions while enjoying significant financial benefits. As a designated 501(c) organization, nonprofits are exempt from paying federal income tax, eligible to receive tax-deductible donations from supporters, and may qualify for various government grants and other funding opportunities. However, the application process can be complex, requiring careful attention to detail and adherence to IRS regulations. This guide will provide a comprehensive overview of the steps involved in applying for 501(c) status for your nonprofit organization, including key requirements, best practices, and tips

for success.

Understand the Eligibility Requirements:

Before applying for 501(c) tax-exempt status, it's crucial to ensure that your nonprofit organization meets the eligibility requirements outlined by the Internal Revenue Service (IRS). Generally, to qualify for 501(c) status, an organization must meet the following criteria:

Organizational Purpose: The primary purpose of the organization must be charitable, religious, educational, scientific, literary, testing for public safety, fostering national or international amateur sports competition, or preventing cruelty to children or animals. The purpose must be clearly stated in the organization's articles of incorporation or governing documents.

Non-Distribution of Earnings: The organization's earnings and assets cannot benefit any individual or private shareholder. All income and assets must be used exclusively for the organization's exempt purposes and activities.

Prohibited Activities: Certain activities are prohibited for 501(c) organizations, including participating in political campaigns, or lobbying activities, engaging in substantial legislative activity, and providing private benefits to individuals or organizations.

Organizational Structure: The organization must be structured as a corporation, trust, or unincorporated association recognized under state law. It must also have a specific dissolution clause in its governing documents, ensuring that its assets are distributed for exempt purposes upon dissolution.

Operational Compliance: The organization must comply with all applicable federal, state, and local laws and regulations governing nonprofit organizations, including filing required reports and disclosures with the IRS and other government agencies.

Before proceeding with the application process, carefully review the eligibility requirements to ensure your organization qualifies for 501(c) tax-exempt status.

Prepare Organizational Documents:

Before applying for 501(c) status, your nonprofit organization must prepare certain organizational documents and governing instruments. These documents will be submitted to the IRS as part of the application process and will provide the foundation for your organization's operations and governance. Key documents to prepare include:

Articles of Incorporation: If your organization is incorporated, you will need to prepare articles of incorporation that comply with state law and include specific language indicating the organization's charitable purposes and Compliance with IRS requirements.

Bylaws: Develop bylaws that outline the internal rules and procedures governing the operation and management of the organization. Include provisions related to board composition, decision-making processes, meetings, and officer roles and responsibilities.

Conflict of Interest Policy: Adopt a conflict-of-interest policy to address and manage conflicts of interest among board members, staff, volunteers, or other stakeholders. Board members must disclose any potential conflicts of interest and abstain from participating in decisions where they have a personal or financial interest.

Ensure that these documents are carefully drafted and reviewed to ensure Compliance with IRS regulations and state laws governing nonprofit organizations.

Complete IRS Form 1023 or Form 1023-EZ:

The next step in applying for 501(c) status is to complete and submit IRS Form 1023, "Application for Recognition of Exemption Under Section 501(c) of the Internal Revenue Code," or Form 1023-EZ, "Streamlined Application for Recognition of Exemption Under Section 501(c) of the Internal Revenue Code." The form you use will depend on the size and complexity of your organization.

Form 1023: Form 1023 is the standard application form for 501(c) status and is suitable for larger organizations with annual gross receipts exceeding $50,000 or assets exceeding $250,000. The form requires detailed information about the organization's history, activities, finances, governance structure, and Compliance with IRS requirements. It also requires a narrative description of the organization's programs and activities and copies of organizational documents, financial statements, and other supporting documentation.

Form 1023-EZ: Form 1023-EZ is a streamlined application form for smaller organizations with annual gross receipts of $50,000 or less and total assets of $250,000 or less. The form is shorter and less complex than Form 1023 and requires basic information about the organization's structure, activities, and finances. However, not all organizations are eligible to use Form 1023-EZ, and certain types of organizations, such as schools, hospitals, and churches, are ineligible.

Carefully review each form's instructions to determine which is appropriate for your organization and ensure that you provide all required information and documentation.

Submit the Application and Pay the Fee:
Once you have completed the appropriate form, apply to the IRS with any required documentation and the applicable user fee. The user fee for Form 1023 is based on the organization's gross receipts and ranges from $275 to $2,000, while the fee for Form 1023-EZ is $275. Payment can be made by check, money order, or credit/debit card, and should be included with the application.

Await IRS Review and Determination:
After submitting the application, the IRS will review the materials and documentation provided and determine the organization's eligibility for 501(c) tax-exempt status. This process can take several months, depending on the volume of applications and the complexity of the organization's structure and activities.

The IRS may request additional information or clarification regarding the organization's activities, finances, or governance structure during the review process. It is important to respond promptly and thoroughly to any requests from the IRS to expedite the review process and ensure a favorable determination.

Receive IRS Determination Letter:
Once the IRS has completed its review, the organization will receive a determination letter indicating whether it has been granted 501(c) tax-exempt status. If approved, the determination letter will include the effective date of tax-exempt status, which is typically retroactive to the date of incorporation or the date the organization was formed.

If the organization's application is denied, the determination letter will provide the reasons for the denial and instructions for appealing the decision, if applicable. In some cases, organizations may be able to address deficiencies or provide additional information to resolve issues and obtain approval for tax-exempt status.

Maintain Compliance:
Once your organization has been granted 501(c) tax-exempt status, it's essential to comply with IRS regulations and reporting requirements. This includes filing annual information returns, such as Form 990, with the IRS and any required state or local filings. Be sure to keep accurate financial records, document your organization's activities and accomplishments, and adhere to any restrictions or limitations imposed by your tax-exempt status.

By staying organized and compliant, you can ensure that your organization continues to enjoy the benefits of 501(c) tax-exempt status while fulfilling its mission and serving its community effectively.

In conclusion, applying for 501(c) tax-exempt status for your nonprofit organization is a significant undertaking that requires careful preparation, attention to detail, and adherence to IRS regulations. By following these steps and best practices, you can navigate the application process successfully and position your organization for long-term success and impact.

Applying for 501(c) tax-exempt status for your nonprofit organization in Atlanta, Georgia involves several steps, including preparing documentation, completing the

application, and submitting it to the IRS. Here's a step-by-step guide on how to apply online for your 501(c) tax-exempt certificate:

Step 1: Gather Required Information:
Before starting the application process, gather all necessary information and documentation. This may include:
Legal name and address of the organization
Employer Identification Number (EIN).
Organizational structure and governance documents (articles of incorporation, bylaws, conflict of interest policy).
Description of the organization's activities and purpose
Financial information, including budget and sources of funding.
Names and contact information of officers, directors, and key personnel.
Ensure you have all the required information and documentation to streamline the application process.

Step 2: Access the IRS Website:
Navigate to the official website of the Internal Revenue Service (IRS) at www.irs.gov using a web browser.

Step 3: Locate the Online Application Portal:
Once on the IRS website, locate the section for applying for tax-exempt status. This can typically be found under the "Charities and Nonprofits" or "Forms & Instructions" section.

Step 4: Choose the Form:
Select the appropriate form for applying for 501(c) tax-exempt status. Depending on your organization's size and complexity, you will usually use Form 1023 or Form 1023-EZ.
Form 1023 is used for larger organizations with gross receipts exceeding $50,000 or assets exceeding $250,000.
Form 1023-EZ: This streamlined form is used for smaller organizations with gross receipts of $50,000 or less and total assets of $250,000 or less.

Step 5: Complete the Online Application:
Follow the instructions provided to complete the online application form. Provide accurate and detailed information about your organization's activities, governance structure, and financials.

Step 6: Submit the Application:
Once you have completed the online application form, please review it carefully to ensure accuracy and completeness. Then, apply electronically through the IRS website.

Step 7: Pay the Fee:
As of the time of writing, the fee for applying for 501(c) tax-exempt status varies depending on the form used and the organization's financial status. Here are the current fees:
Form 1023: The fee for Form 1023 ranges from $275 to $2,000, based on the organization's gross receipts over the past three years.
Form 1023-EZ: The fee for Form 1023-EZ is a flat $275.
Ensure you have the necessary funds to pay the fee online using a credit or debit card.

Step 8: Await IRS Review and Determination:
After submitting the application and fee, the IRS will review the materials and documentation provided. This process can take several months, so be patient and await communication from the IRS.

Step 9: Receive IRS Determination Letter:
Once the IRS has reviewed your application, you will receive a determination letter indicating whether your organization has been granted 501(c) tax-exempt status. If approved, the determination letter will include the effective date of tax-exempt status.

Step 10: Maintain Compliance:

After receiving tax-exempt status, it's important to maintain Compliance with IRS regulations and reporting requirements. This includes filing annual information returns (Form 990) and adhering to any restrictions or limitations imposed by your tax-exempt status.

Following these steps and staying organized throughout the application process, you can apply online for your nonprofit organization's 501(c)(3) tax-exempt certificate in Atlanta, Georgia.

CHAPTER 10

Register with State Authorities

Applying for and obtaining necessary licenses and permits is a critical step for nonprofit 501(c) tax-exempt organizations to ensure compliance with legal and regulatory requirements. These licenses and permits may vary depending on the organization's activities, location, and the laws and regulations governing its operations. In this comprehensive guide, we will explore the process of applying for and obtaining necessary licenses and permits for your nonprofit organization, covering key steps, considerations, and examples of commonly required licenses and permits.

Identify Required Licenses and Permits:
The first step in obtaining necessary licenses and permits for your nonprofit organization is to identify the required licenses and permits based on your organization's activities and location. Standard licenses and permits that nonprofit organizations may need to obtain include:

Business License: Many cities and counties require businesses, including nonprofit organizations, to obtain a business license to operate legally within their jurisdiction. This license typically covers general business activities and may be required regardless of the organization's tax-exempt status.

Charitable Solicitation License: Nonprofit organizations engaged in fundraising activities and soliciting donations from the public may need to obtain a charitable solicitation license or registration from the state government or relevant authorities. This license ensures that the organization complies with fundraising regulations and protects donors from fraudulent or deceptive practices.

Tax Exemption Certificate: While nonprofit organizations with 501(c) tax-exempt status are generally exempt from federal income tax, they may still need to obtain a tax exemption certificate or letter from the state tax authority to exempt them from certain state and local taxes, such as sales tax or property tax.

Professional Licenses: Nonprofit organizations that provide certain professional services, such as healthcare, legal, or educational services, may need professional licenses or certifications for staff members or volunteers, depending on state licensing requirements.

Special Event Permits: If your organization plans to host special events, such as fundraising galas, festivals, or concerts, you may need special event permits from local authorities to ensure compliance with zoning regulations, health and safety standards, and other requirements.

Identifying the licenses and permits required for your nonprofit organization will depend on its activities, location, and legal requirements governing its operations.

Research Regulatory Requirements:

Once you have identified the licenses and permits for your nonprofit organization, research the regulatory requirements and application procedures for each license or permit. This may involve:

Consulting Government Websites: Visit the websites of relevant government agencies, such as state and local revenue departments, business licensing offices, or charitable solicitation regulators, to access information and resources on licensing requirements and procedures.

Reviewing State Laws and Regulations: Familiarize yourself with state laws and regulations governing nonprofit organizations, charitable solicitation, and other relevant activities to ensure compliance with legal requirements.

Seeking Legal Advice: Consider consulting with legal counsel or advisors familiar with nonprofit law and regulatory compliance to clarify any questions or concerns about licensing requirements and application procedures.

Gathering information about regulatory requirements and procedures will help ensure that your organization submits complete and accurate license and permit applications and avoids potential delays or compliance issues.

Prepare Required Documentation:

Before applying for licenses and permits, gather the necessary documentation and information to support your applications. Standard documents and information that may be required include:

Organization Information: Provide basic information about your nonprofit organization, including its legal name, address, contact information, and tax identification number (EIN).

Governing Documents: To demonstrate your organization's legal and tax-exempt status, submit copies of its governing documents, such as articles of incorporation, bylaws, and tax exemption certificates from the IRS.

Financial Statements: Depending on the type of license or permit, you may need to provide financial statements or documentation demonstrating your organization's financial stability and ability to meet licensing requirements.

Background Checks: Some licenses or permits may require background checks for staff members, volunteers, or board members, particularly for roles involving vulnerable populations or sensitive activities.

Event Plans: If applying for special event permits, provide detailed event plans, including dates, locations, activities, safety measures, and any other relevant information requested by local authorities.

To streamline the process and avoid delays, ensure you have all required documentation prepared and organized before submitting your license and permit applications.

Complete License and Permit Applications:
Once you have gathered the necessary documentation, complete the license and permit applications according to the instructions provided by the issuing authorities. Be sure to:

Provide Accurate Information: Fill out the application forms wholly and accurately, ensuring all required fields are filled in and all requested information is provided.

Follow Instructions: Read the application instructions carefully and follow any specific guidelines or requirements provided by the issuing authorities, such as submission deadlines, application fees, or supporting documentation.

Submit Required Fees: Include any required application fees or payments with your license and permit applications, either by check, money order, or electronic payment, as specified by the issuing authorities.

Retain Copies: Make copies of all completed license and permit applications, supporting documentation, and payment receipts for your records before submitting them to the issuing authorities.

Submitting complete and accurate license and permit applications will help expedite the review process and increase the likelihood of approval for your nonprofit organization.

Await Review and Approval:
After submitting your license and permit applications, you must await review and approval from the issuing authorities. The processing time for license and permit applications may vary depending on factors such as the complexity of the application, the volume of applications received, and the responsiveness of the issuing authorities.

During the review process, the issuing authorities may conduct inspections, background checks, or other assessments to verify your organization's eligibility and compliance with licensing requirements. To facilitate the review process, be prepared to provide additional information or address any concerns or questions raised by the issuing authorities promptly.

Maintain Compliance and Renewals:
Once your nonprofit organization has obtained the necessary licenses and permits, it's essential to maintain compliance with all applicable regulations and requirements. This may include:

Renewing Licenses and Permits: Monitor the expiration dates of your organization's licenses and permits and ensure timely renewal to avoid interruptions in operations or compliance issues.

Adhering to Regulations: Stay informed about any changes to licensing requirements, regulations, or industry standards that may affect your organization's operations and ensure ongoing compliance with all applicable laws and regulations.

Recordkeeping: Keep accurate and up-to-date records of your organization's licenses, permits, and related documentation, including renewal dates, application forms, supporting documentation, and payment receipts, for easy reference and audit purposes.

By maintaining compliance with licensing requirements and regulations, your nonprofit organization can operate legally and effectively, uphold its reputation, and fulfill its mission while serving its beneficiaries and stakeholders.

Examples of Commonly Required Licenses and Permits for Nonprofit Organizations:
To provide further context, here are examples of commonly required licenses and permits for nonprofit organizations:

Business License: Many cities and counties require business licenses for operating businesses, including nonprofit organizations, within their jurisdiction.

Charitable Solicitation License: This license is required for fundraising activities, such as soliciting donations from the public, to ensure compliance with fundraising regulations and protect donors from fraudulent or deceptive practices.

Tax Exemption Certificate: Issued by state tax authorities to exempt nonprofit organizations from certain state and local taxes, such as sales tax or property tax, based.

Let's walk through the step-by-step process of how a nonprofit 501(c) tax-exempt organization in Atlanta, Georgia, can apply to obtain the necessary licenses and permits:

Step 1: Identify Required Licenses and Permits:

Begin by identifying the licenses and permits required for your nonprofit organization based on its activities and location in Atlanta, Georgia. Standard licenses and permits may include:

Business License: Required for operating a business, including nonprofit organizations, within Atlanta.

Charitable Solicitation License: This license is needed for fundraising activities, such as soliciting donations from the public, to comply with state regulations.

Tax Exemption Certificate: Issued by the Georgia Department of Revenue to exempt nonprofit organizations from certain state taxes.

Research the regulatory requirements and determine which licenses and permits are necessary for your organization's operations.

Step 2: Research Regulatory Requirements:

Next, research the regulatory requirements and application procedures for each required license and permit. This may involve:

Visit the City of Atlanta's official website to access business licensing requirements and procedures information.

Review the Georgia Secretary of State's website for information on charitable solicitation registration requirements and procedures.

Consult the Georgia Department of Revenue's website for guidance on obtaining a tax exemption certificate.

Familiarize yourself with the relevant laws, regulations, and procedures governing nonprofit organizations in Atlanta,

Georgia.

Step 3: Prepare Required Documentation:

Gather the necessary documentation and information to support your license and permit applications. This may include:

Organization Information: Legal name, address, contact information, and tax identification number (EIN) of your nonprofit organization.

Governing Documents: Copies of articles of incorporation, bylaws, and IRS determination letter confirming tax-exempt status.

Financial Statements: Documentation demonstrating your organization's financial stability and ability to meet licensing requirements.

Background Checks: If required, background checks are performed on staff members, volunteers, or board members involved in fundraising activities.

Ensure all required documentation is accurate, up-to-date, and organized for submission with your applications.

Step 4: Complete License and Permit Applications:

Fill out the application forms for each required license and permit according to the instructions provided by the issuing authorities. Be sure to:

Provide accurate information and complete all the necessary fields on the application forms.

Follow any specific guidelines or requirements provided by the issuing authorities.

Include any required application fees with your submissions.

Submit your completed license and permit applications and the necessary documentation to the appropriate authorities.

Step 5: Await Review and Approval:

After submitting your applications, you must await review and approval from the issuing authorities. The processing time may vary depending on the complexity of the applications and the volume of submissions.

During the review process, be prepared to respond promptly to any inquiries or requests for additional information from the issuing authorities.

Step 6: Maintain Compliance and Renewals:

Once your nonprofit organization has obtained the necessary licenses and permits, it's essential to maintain compliance with all applicable regulations and requirements. This includes:

Renewing licenses and permits before they expire to ensure continuous compliance and operations.

Staying informed about any changes to licensing requirements or regulations that may affect your organization.

Keeping accurate records of all licenses, permits, and related documentation for reference and audit purposes.

By following these steps and staying proactive in maintaining compliance, your nonprofit organization can operate legally and effectively while fulfilling its mission in Atlanta, Georgia.

CHAPTER 11

Develop Policies and Procedures

Developing policies and procedures for your nonprofit 501(c) tax-exempt organization is essential for ensuring transparency, accountability, and compliance with legal and regulatory requirements. Policies and procedures guide staff, volunteers, and board members on how the organization operates, makes decisions, and manages its resources. In this comprehensive guide, we will explore the process of developing effective policies and procedures for your nonprofit organization, covering key steps, best practices, and examples of commonly implemented policies.

Understand the Importance of Policies and Procedures:
Before diving into the development process, it's essential to understand why policies and procedures are crucial for nonprofit organizations:

Compliance: Policies and procedures help ensure compliance with legal and regulatory requirements, including IRS regulations for maintaining tax-exempt status.

Transparency: Clear policies and procedures promote transparency and accountability by outlining how the organization operates and makes decisions.

Risk Management: Well-defined policies and procedures help mitigate risks by establishing financial management, governance, and operations guidelines.

Consistency: Policies and procedures promote consistency in decision-making and operations, reducing confusion and potential conflicts.

Efficiency: Standardized processes streamline operations and improve efficiency by providing clear guidelines for staff and volunteers.

By developing comprehensive policies and procedures, nonprofit organizations can strengthen their governance practices, enhance organizational effectiveness, and build stakeholder trust.

Identify Areas Requiring Policies and Procedures:
The first step in developing policies and procedures is to identify the areas of your organization that require documentation. Common areas that may require policies and procedures include:

Governance: Establish policies governing the structure and responsibilities of the board of directors, including board composition, meetings, and decision-making processes.

Financial Management: Develop policies and procedures for budgeting, financial reporting, cash management, and internal controls to ensure proper stewardship of the organization's resources.

Human Resources: Create policies related to hiring, compensation, benefits, performance evaluation, and employee conduct to promote a positive work environment and ensure compliance with employment laws.

Program Operations: Develop policies and procedures for program development, implementation, evaluation, and reporting to ensure that programs align with the organization's mission and achieve desired outcomes.

Fundraising and Development: Establish guidelines for

fundraising activities, donor stewardship, gift acceptance, and compliance with fundraising regulations to maintain donor trust and support.

Risk Management: Develop policies and procedures for managing risks related to legal compliance, conflicts of interest, data security, and insurance coverage to protect the organization and its stakeholders.

Board Governance: Define the board of directors' roles and responsibilities, including meeting protocols, conflict of interest policies, and board member expectations.

Identifying these areas will help ensure that your organization's policies and procedures cover all critical aspects of its operations and governance.

Conduct a Policy Review and Gap Analysis:

Once you've identified the areas requiring policies and procedures, conduct a comprehensive review of your organization's existing policies, if any, and assess any gaps or deficiencies. This may involve:

Reviewing Existing Policies: Examine existing policies and procedures to determine their relevance, effectiveness, and compliance with legal and regulatory requirements.

Identifying Gaps: Identify areas where policies and procedures are lacking, or outdated or new policies are needed to address emerging issues or risks.

Consulting Stakeholders: Seek input from key stakeholders, including board members, staff, volunteers, and external advisors, to identify areas of concern or where policies and procedures could be improved.

Conducting a thorough policy review and gap analysis will provide a solid foundation for developing new policies and updating existing ones to meet the organization's needs and objectives.

Develop Draft Policies and Procedures:

Based on the policy review and gap analysis findings, develop draft policies and procedures for each identified area. When developing policies and procedures, consider the following best practices:

Clear and Concise Language: Use clear, concise language easily understood by all stakeholders, avoiding technical jargon or complex terminology.

Alignment with Mission and Values: Ensure that policies and procedures align with the organization's mission, values, and strategic objectives, reflecting its commitment to ethical conduct and accountability.

Legal and Regulatory Compliance: Ensure policies and procedures comply with applicable laws, regulations, and industry standards, including IRS regulations for tax-exempt organizations.

Flexibility and Adaptability: Design policies and procedures to be flexible and adaptable to accommodate changes in the organization's operations, external environment, and emerging risks.

Accessibility: Make policies and procedures accessible to all stakeholders by maintaining a centralized repository, such as an employee handbook or online portal, and providing training on their use and implementation.

Feedback and Review: Solicit input from stakeholders on draft policies and procedures to ensure that they meet their needs and address any concerns or questions. Periodically review and update policies and procedures to reflect changes in the organization's operations or regulatory requirements.

Developing draft policies and procedures may involve collaboration with staff, board members, and subject matter experts to ensure they are comprehensive, practical, and effective.

CHAPTER 12

Start Operations

Starting operations for your nonprofit 501(c) tax-exempt organization involves a comprehensive process encompassing various steps, from setting up administrative infrastructure to launching programs and fundraising initiatives. In this detailed guide, we'll explore each aspect of starting operations for your nonprofit organization, covering key considerations, best practices, and actionable steps to ensure a successful launch and sustainable growth.

Establish Administrative Infrastructure:
The first step in starting operations for your nonprofit organization is establishing the administrative infrastructure necessary to support its activities. This includes:

Governance Structure:
Define your organization's governance structure, including the board of directors, officers, and committees. Ensure that roles and responsibilities are clearly defined and aligned with the organization's mission and objectives.

Bylaws and Policies:
Draft and adopt bylaws that outline the rules and procedures governing the operation and management of the organization. Develop critical policies, such as conflict of interest, code of

conduct, and whistleblower policies, to promote transparency, accountability, and ethical conduct.

Financial Management:
Set up financial management systems and procedures to ensure proper stewardship of the organization's resources. Establish a budget, accounting system, and internal controls to manage finances effectively and comply with regulatory requirements.

Legal Compliance:
Ensure compliance with all legal and regulatory requirements governing nonprofit organizations, including tax-exempt status, charitable solicitation, and reporting obligations. Obtain necessary licenses, permits, and registrations from federal, state, and local authorities.

Technology and Infrastructure:
Invest in technology and infrastructure to support organizational operations, communication, and collaboration. This may include setting up a website, email accounts, and software tools for project management, fundraising, and donor management.

Develop Programs and Services:
Once the administrative infrastructure is in place, focus on developing programs and services that align with your organization's mission and address the needs of your target beneficiaries. This involves:

Needs Assessment:
Conduct a needs assessment to identify the specific needs and challenges your target population or community faces. Gather data through surveys, focus groups, and research to inform program development.

Program Design:
Design programs and services responsive to identified needs and aligned with the organization's mission and strategic priorities. Define program goals, objectives, activities, and evaluation

measures to track progress and outcomes.

Partnership Development:
Collaborate with other organizations, community groups, and stakeholders to leverage resources, expertise, and networks. Form partnerships and alliances that enhance the effectiveness and reach of your programs and services.

Volunteer Recruitment and Training:
Recruit volunteers who are passionate about your organization's mission and can contribute their time, skills, and expertise to support program delivery. Provide training and orientation to volunteers to ensure they can effectively fulfill their roles.

Implement Fundraising and Revenue Generation Strategies:
To sustain operations and support programmatic activities, develop fundraising and revenue generation strategies tailored to your organization's mission, target audience, and capacity. This includes:

Diversified Fundraising Channels:
Explore a variety of fundraising channels, including individual donations, grants, corporate sponsorships, events, and earned income streams. Diversifying revenue sources helps mitigate risks and ensure financial stability.

Grant Writing and Proposal Development:
Identify grant opportunities from foundations, government agencies, and other funders that align with your organization's programs and priorities. Develop compelling grant proposals that clearly articulate your initiatives' needs, Impact, and sustainability.

Donor Cultivation and Stewardship:
Cultivate relationships with donors, supporters, and stakeholders through personalized communication, engagement opportunities, and recognition initiatives. Practice donor stewardship to express gratitude, provide updates on Impact and

nurture long-term relationships.

Fundraising Events and Campaigns:
Organize fundraising events, campaigns, and appeals to mobilize support and raise awareness about your organization's mission and programs. Plan and execute events that are creative, engaging, and aligned with your fundraising goals.

Build Community Engagement and Awareness:
Engage with the community and raise awareness about your organization's mission, programs, and Impact. This involves:

Outreach and Advocacy:
Engage in outreach and advocacy efforts to educate the public, policymakers, and stakeholders about key issues and solutions related to your organization's mission. Advocate for policy changes and systemic reforms that support your objectives.

Public Relations and Media Outreach:
Develop a public relations strategy to generate media coverage, press releases, and social media content that highlight your organization's achievements, milestones, and stories of Impact. Build relationships with journalists, influencers, and media outlets to amplify your message.

Community Events and Activities:
Participate in community events, forums, and activities to connect with residents, businesses, and organizations in your area. Host workshops, seminars, and informational sessions to share knowledge, resources, and best practices with the community.

Online Engagement and Social Media:
Harness the power of digital platforms and social media channels to engage with supporters, volunteers, and stakeholders. Maintain an active online presence, share updates, stories, and calls to action, and foster dialogue and interaction with your audience.

Monitor and Evaluate Impact:

Monitor and evaluate the Impact of your organization's programs and activities to assess effectiveness, identify areas for improvement, and demonstrate accountability to stakeholders. This involves:

Data Collection and Analysis:
Collect data and metrics related to program outcomes, outputs, and indicators using qualitative and quantitative methods. Analyze data to track progress, measure impact, and inform decision-making.

Performance Measurement:
Develop performance metrics and key indicators (KPIs) to evaluate program performance and organizational effectiveness. Establish benchmarks and targets to assess progress toward goals and objectives.

Stakeholder Feedback:
Solicit feedback from beneficiaries, clients, volunteers, donors, and other stakeholders to gather insights, perspectives, and suggestions for improvement. Use feedback to inform programmatic decisions and enhance service delivery.

Impact Reporting and Communication:
Prepare impact reports, annual reports, and presentations communicating the organization's achievements, outcomes, and Impact to stakeholders. Share success stories, testimonials, and data-driven evidence to demonstrate the value and effectiveness of your organization's work.

By following these steps and adopting a strategic and systematic approach, your nonprofit 501(c) tax-exempt organization can start operations effectively, deliver meaningful programs and services, engage with the community, and achieve its mission and objectives.

CHAPTER 13

Setting up for success as a nonprofit

Setting up for success as a nonprofit organization involves laying a solid foundation rooted in a clear vision, strategic planning, and targeted engagement with key stakeholders. By focusing on your organization's vision and identifying target audiences, you can effectively align your activities, build meaningful partnerships, and create impactful programs that benefit your organization and the communities you serve. In this comprehensive guide, we will explore the essential steps and strategies for setting up a nonprofit organization for success, with a particular emphasis on vision, target audiences, and community engagement.

Define Your Vision and Mission:
At the heart of every successful nonprofit organization is a compelling vision and mission that inspires action and drives impact. Begin by defining your organization's vision, which is a statement that articulates the future you aspire to create. Your vision should be ambitious yet achievable and reflect your organization's core values and principles. Once you have a clear vision, develop a mission statement that succinctly communicates the purpose and objectives of your organization. Your mission statement should answer the following questions: What is the problem or issue your organization seeks to address?

Who are the beneficiaries or target populations you aim to serve?
What are the primary activities or interventions your organization will undertake?
What are the desired outcomes or impacts you hope to achieve?
By defining a compelling vision and mission, you provide a guiding framework for your organization's activities and inspire stakeholders to support your cause.

Identify Target Audiences and Stakeholders:
To effectively reach and engage with your target audiences, it's essential to identify and understand the diverse stakeholders who have a vested interest in your organization's mission and work. Consider the following key stakeholders:
Beneficiaries: The individuals or communities directly impacted by your organization's programs and services. Identify their needs, preferences, and challenges to tailor your interventions effectively.
Donors and Funders are individuals, foundations, corporations, and government agencies that financially support your organization. Understand their funding priorities, motivations, and grantmaking criteria to cultivate meaningful relationships.
Partners and Collaborators: Other nonprofit organizations, government agencies, businesses, academic institutions, and community groups with similar goals and objectives. Identify opportunities for collaboration, resource sharing, and collective Impact.
Volunteers and Supporters are individuals who contribute their time, skills, and resources to support your organization's activities. By providing meaningful opportunities for involvement and recognition, you can cultivate a sense of belonging and engagement among volunteers and supporters.

By understanding the needs, interests, and motivations of your target audiences and stakeholders, you can tailor your communication and engagement strategies to mobilize support and drive impact effectively.

Establish Strategic Partnerships and Collaborations:
Collaboration is key to the success of nonprofit organizations, as it enables them to leverage resources, expertise, and networks to achieve common goals and maximize Impact. Identify potential partners and collaborators who share your organization's vision and can contribute complementary strengths and resources. Consider the following strategies for establishing strategic partnerships:

Research and Outreach: Conduct research to identify potential partners and collaborators in your field or community. Contact them to explore opportunities for collaboration and discuss shared goals and objectives.

Memorandums of Understanding (MOUs): Formalize partnerships and collaborations through written agreements, such as MOUs or partnership agreements. Clearly define roles, responsibilities, and expectations to ensure mutual understanding and accountability.

Joint Programs and Initiatives: Develop joint programs, initiatives, or projects with partner organizations to address common challenges and achieve shared objectives. Pool resources, expertise, and networks to enhance program effectiveness and sustainability.

Networking and Relationship Building: Attend networking events, conferences, and meetings within your sector or community to build relationships with potential partners and collaborators. Engage in meaningful conversations, share insights, and explore opportunities for collaboration.

By forging strategic partnerships and collaborations, your organization can amplify its Impact, reach new audiences, and achieve greater sustainability and scalability.

Engage with Target Audiences and Stakeholders:
Effective engagement with target audiences and stakeholders is essential for building support, mobilizing resources, and driving Impact. Consider the following strategies for engaging with your target audiences and stakeholders:

Direct Outreach and Communication: Reach out to target audiences and stakeholders through personalized communication channels, such as emails, newsletters, and social media platforms. Tailor you're messaging to resonate with their interests, values, and priorities.

Community Events and Activities: Host community events, workshops, seminars, and informational sessions to engage with target audiences and stakeholders in person. Provide dialogue, feedback, and participation opportunities to foster a sense of ownership and belonging.

Participatory Decision-Making: Involve target audiences and stakeholders in decision-making processes, program design, and strategic planning. Seek their input, feedback, and perspectives to ensure your organization's activities respond to their needs and preferences.

Advocacy and Empowerment: Advocate for policies, programs, and resources that benefit your target populations and communities. Empower target audiences and stakeholders to advocate for themselves and participate in advocacy efforts to drive systemic change.

By engaging with target audiences and stakeholders, your organization can build trust, credibility, and support, driving greater awareness, participation, and Impact.

Measure and Communicate Impact:

Measuring and communicating Impact is essential for demonstrating accountability, transparency, and effectiveness. Develop systems and processes for monitoring and evaluating your organization's programs and activities. Collect data, metrics, and feedback to assess progress toward goals and outcomes. Analyze findings to identify strengths, weaknesses, and areas for improvement. Communicate Impact to stakeholders through various channels, including impact reports, annual reports, case studies, and testimonials. Share success stories, testimonials, and data-driven evidence to illustrate your organization's difference in the lives of beneficiaries and communities. Engage stakeholders in dialogue and reflection on lessons learned, best practices, and future directions. By measuring and communicating Impact effectively, your organization can build credibility, inspire confidence, and attract support from donors, funders, partners, and stakeholders.

Conclusion: Setting up for success as a nonprofit organization requires a strategic approach rooted in vision, target audience identification, and community engagement. By defining a compelling vision, identifying target audiences and stakeholders, establishing strategic partnerships, engaging with communities, and measuring Impact, your organization can create meaningful change, drive sustainable growth, and achieve its mission and objectives through strategic planning, collaboration, and continuous learning.

CHAPTER 14

The secret to applying for government and corporate grants in this digital age!

Starting a nonprofit organization is a noble endeavor that requires careful planning, strategic thinking, and dedication to your mission. While the first year may pose challenges, it also presents opportunities for growth and impact. This comprehensive guide will delve into the secrets of applying for government and corporate grants, navigating the initial stages of nonprofit operation, and ensuring financial sustainability for your organization.

Lay the Foundation:
Before seeking grants, it's essential to establish a solid foundation for your nonprofit organization. This includes:
Defining Your Mission and Vision: Clearly articulate your organization's purpose and objectives, aligning them with the needs of your target beneficiaries and communities.
Incorporating Your Organization: File articles of incorporation with the state and obtain tax-exempt status from the IRS under section 501(c)(3) of the Internal Revenue Code.
Setting Up Administrative Systems: Establish administrative systems for governance, financial management, and compliance with legal and regulatory requirements.

Opening a Bank Account: Open a separate bank account for your nonprofit to track donations, manage finances, and demonstrate financial transparency.

Self-Funding and Visibility:
In the early stages, self-funding may be necessary to cover startup costs and initial expenses. However, focus on activities that enhance your visibility and credibility within the community:
Invest in Marketing and Outreach: Promote your organization's mission and programs through social media, networking events, and community partnerships to raise awareness and attract supporters.
Highlight Your Tax-Exempt Status: Emphasize your 501(c)(3) tax-exempt status when soliciting donations, assuring donors that their contributions are tax-deductible.
Maintain Financial Records: Keep detailed records of all income and expenditures to ensure transparency and accountability, which are essential for grant applications and IRS compliance.

Develop a Comprehensive Business Plan:
A well-crafted business plan is a roadmap for your organization's growth and sustainability. Include the following elements:
Mission and Goals: Clearly define your organization's mission, goals, and objectives, outlining the impact you seek to achieve in the community.
Programs and Services: Describe the programs and services your organization will offer and explain how they address the needs of your target beneficiaries.
Marketing and Fundraising Strategies: Outline strategies for marketing, outreach, and fundraising, identifying target donors, grant opportunities, and revenue streams.
Financial Projections: Develop financial projections, including revenue sources, expenses, and cash flow projections, to demonstrate your organization's financial viability.

Seek Government and Corporate Grants:

Government and corporate grants can provide significant funding to support your organization's programs and initiatives. Follow these steps to secure grants successfully:

Research Grant Opportunities: Identify government agencies, foundations, and corporations that offer grants aligned with your organization's mission and programs.

Read Grant Guidelines: Carefully review the eligibility criteria, application guidelines, and deadlines for each grant opportunity to ensure compliance with requirements.

Develop a Compelling Proposal: Craft a persuasive grant proposal that clearly articulates your organization's mission, goals, and programs. The proposal should demonstrate the need for funding and the expected impact of your initiatives.

Provide Supporting Documentation: To strengthen your grant application, include supporting documentation such as financial statements, program budgets, and organizational credentials.

Follow-Up: After submitting your proposal, follow up with Grantmakers to inquire about the status of your application and address any additional information or documentation required.

Ensure Compliance and Accountability:

Maintaining compliance with IRS regulations and reporting requirements is essential for nonprofit organizations. Here's how to stay on track:

File Annual Reports: Submit Form 990 or 990-EZ to the IRS annually, providing information about your organization's finances, activities, and governance.

Comply with Reporting Obligations: Fulfill reporting obligations to Grantmakers, government agencies, and regulatory authorities, providing updates on program outcomes, financial performance, and organizational developments.

Implement Internal Controls: Establish internal controls and procedures to safeguard assets, prevent fraud, and ensure the integrity of financial reporting.

Engage in Succession Planning: Develop a succession plan to ensure smooth transitions in leadership and governance. Identify potential successors and provide training and mentorship opportunities.

Conclusion:

Starting and sustaining a nonprofit organization requires vision, determination, and strategic planning. By laying a solid foundation, cultivating visibility and support, developing comprehensive business, and fundraising strategies, and maintaining compliance and accountability, your organization can overcome challenges and thrive in its mission to positively impact the community. Remember, perseverance and adaptability are key as you navigate the dynamic landscape of nonprofit management and grant-seeking. With dedication and resilience, your organization can achieve its goals and create lasting change for the betterment of society.

CHAPTER 15

Artificial intelligence in the nonprofit sector

Incorporating artificial intelligence into the nonprofit sector can revolutionize how organizations define their mission and vision and engage with their target audience. Leveraging ChatGPT as a tool can aid nonprofits in crafting compelling mission and vision statements that resonate with stakeholders while guiding them with keywords and phrases to reach their target audience effectively.

Crafting Your Mission and Vision:

ChatGPT can assist nonprofits in articulating their mission and vision statements by generating ideas, refining language, and ensuring alignment with organizational goals. Here's how:

Idea Generation: ChatGPT can brainstorm ideas based on input provided by nonprofit leaders, such as the organization's purpose, values, and desired impact. By analyzing this information, ChatGPT can suggest mission and vision statements that encapsulate the essence of the organization's work.

Language Refinement: ChatGPT can refine the language of mission and vision statements to make them clear, concise, and impactful. By generating multiple iterations and providing feedback on each, ChatGPT can help nonprofits compellingly articulate their goals.

Alignment with Goals: ChatGPT can ensure that mission and vision statements align with the organization's goals, values, and strategic priorities. By analyzing the organization's objectives and desired outcomes, ChatGPT can suggest language that reflects these aspirations.

Guiding Target Audience Engagement:
Once mission and vision statements are established, ChatGPT can help nonprofits refine their messaging and strategies to effectively engage with their target audience. Here's how:
Keyword Identification: ChatGPT can identify keywords and phrases that resonate with the organization's target audience. By analyzing demographic data, social media trends, and audience preferences, ChatGPT can suggest keywords and phrases that capture the attention of potential supporters.
Tailored Messaging: ChatGPT can assist nonprofits in tailoring their messaging to different segments of their target audience. By generating personalized content based on audience demographics, interests, and preferences, ChatGPT can help nonprofits create engaging and relevant communication materials.
Strategic Outreach: ChatGPT can recommend strategic outreach tactics to reach the organization's target audience. ChatGPT can suggest outreach strategies that maximize impact and visibility by analyzing data on audience behavior and communication channels.

Incorporating ChatGPT into Nonprofit Operations:
Leveraging ChatGPT effectively, nonprofits should integrate it into their operational processes and decision-making frameworks. Here's how:
Training and Integration: Nonprofit staff should undergo training on using ChatGPT effectively and integrating it into their workflow. By familiarizing themselves with ChatGPT's capabilities and limitations, staff can leverage it as a valuable tool in mission-driven work.

Continuous Improvement: Nonprofits should continuously evaluate and refine their use of ChatGPT based on feedback and results. By analyzing data on mission and vision development, target audience engagement, and organizational outcomes, nonprofits can optimize their use of ChatGPT over time.

Ethical Considerations: Nonprofits should consider ethical implications when using ChatGPT, particularly about data privacy, algorithmic bias, and transparency. By adopting ethical guidelines and best practices, nonprofits can ensure responsible and equitable use of ChatGPT in their operations.

Incorporating ChatGPT into nonprofit operations can enhance mission and vision development, guide target audience engagement, and support strategic decision-making. By leveraging ChatGPT's capabilities, nonprofits can amplify their impact and achieve their goals more effectively in the digital age.

CHAPTER 16

How to make your nonprofit visible

Creating visibility for your nonprofit organization is crucial for attracting supporters, engaging with your community, and advancing your mission. In this comprehensive guide, we'll explore step-by-step strategies for making your nonprofit visible, both online and offline, reaching a wider audience, and maximizing your impact.

Step 1: Define Your Brand Identity:
Develop a clear and compelling brand identity that reflects your nonprofit's mission, values, and personality.
Create a memorable logo, color scheme, and visual elements representing your organization.
Craft a compelling tagline or slogan that encapsulates your mission and resonates with your target audience.**Step 2: Build a Professional Website:**
Design and launch a professional website as the central hub for your nonprofit's online presence.
Ensure your website is user-friendly, mobile-responsive, and optimized for search engines (SEO).
Include essential information such as your mission, programs, impact, donation options, and contact details.**Step 3: Leverage Social Media Platforms:**
Identify the social media platforms where your target audience is most active and create profiles for your nonprofit.

Develop a content calendar and consistently share engaging posts, photos, videos, and stories that showcase your work and impact.

Engage with your followers by responding to comments, messages, and inquiries promptly and authentically.

Step 4: Create Compelling Content:

Produce high-quality content that educates, inspires, and motivates your audience to take action.

Share stories, testimonials, case studies, and impact reports highlighting the difference your nonprofit is making in the community.

To appeal to different audience preferences, use a variety of formats, including blog posts, articles, infographics, podcasts, and videos.

Step 5: Implement Email Marketing:

Build an email list of supporters, donors, volunteers, and other stakeholders who have opted in to receive communications from your nonprofit.

Send regular newsletters, updates, and appeals that provide valuable information, highlight upcoming events, and encourage engagement.

Personalize your email campaigns based on recipient interests, preferences, and organizational interactions.

Step 6: Engage with Influencers and Partners:

Identify influencers, thought leaders, and organizations in your field or community who share similar values and interests.

Collaborate with influencers and partners on joint campaigns, events, and initiatives to amplify your reach and impact.

Leverage their networks, expertise, and resources to raise awareness, attract supporters, and drive engagement.**Step 7: Participate in Community Events and Activities:**

Attending local community events, fairs, festivals, and conferences to connect with members of your community and raise awareness about your nonprofit.

Host your events, such as fundraisers, workshops, volunteer

days, and awareness campaigns, to engage with supporters and showcase your work.

Partner with local businesses, schools, churches, and civic organizations to co-host events and reach new audiences.

Step 8: Cultivate Relationships with Media Outlets:

Develop relationships with journalists, reporters, bloggers, and influencers who cover topics relevant to your nonprofit's mission and work.

Pitch story ideas, press releases, and media advisories to local and national media outlets to generate positive coverage and raise awareness about your organization.

Offer expert commentary, insights, or guest posts on relevant issues or current events.

Step 9: Measure and Evaluate Impact:

Track and analyze key performance indicators (KPIs) such as website traffic, social media engagement, email open rates, and donation conversions to measure the effectiveness of your visibility efforts.

Use analytics tools and metrics to identify trends, patterns, and areas for improvement, adjusting your strategies and tactics accordingly.

Solicit feedback from your audience, volunteers, donors, and partners to gauge perception and satisfaction with your nonprofit's visibility and communications.

Step 10: Continuously Improve and Innovate:

Stay informed about emerging trends, technologies, and best practices in nonprofit marketing, communications, and visibility.

Experiment with new strategies, platforms, and tactics to keep your nonprofit's visibility fresh, relevant, and engaging.

Solicit input from your team, board members, volunteers, and supporters to generate new ideas and approaches for increasing visibility and impact.

By following these step-by-step strategies, you can effectively make your nonprofit visible, expand your reach, engage your audience, and advance your mission meaningfully.

CHAPTER 17

Using Social Media to Promote Your Nonprofit

Harnessing the power of social media is essential for promoting your nonprofit organization, engaging with your community, and advancing your mission. This comprehensive guide will explore step-by-step strategies and best practices for effectively leveraging social media to raise awareness, attract supporters, and drive action for your nonprofit.

Understanding the Social Media Landscape
1.1 The Importance of Social Media for Nonprofits
Explore why social media is a powerful tool for nonprofits, including its ability to reach a broad audience, drive engagement, and amplify your impact.
Understand the role of different social media platforms and how they can complement your organization's goals and objectives.

1.2 Key Social Media Platforms for Nonprofits
Dive into the significant social media platforms nonprofits use, including Facebook, Instagram, Twitter, LinkedIn, and YouTube.
Learn about each platform's unique features, audience demographics, and best practices to optimize your presence and engagement.

Developing a Social Media Strategy

2.1 Setting Clear Goals and Objectives

Define your nonprofit's social media goals and objectives, aligning them with your organization's mission, values, and strategic priorities.

Establish measurable metrics and key performance indicators (KPIs) to track progress and evaluate the effectiveness of your social media efforts.

2.2 Identifying Your Target Audience

Identify and segment your target audience based on demographics, interests, behaviors, and preferences.

Tailor your content, messaging, and engagement strategies to resonate with different audience segments and foster meaningful connections.

2.3 Crafting Compelling Content

Develop a content strategy that compellingly and authentically showcases your nonprofit's mission, impact, and programs.

To capture and maintain audience attention, create diverse and engaging content formats, including posts, stories, videos, graphics, and user-generated content.

2.4 Establishing a Consistent Brand Identity

Define your nonprofit's brand voice, tone, and visual identity across all social media platforms to maintain consistency and authenticity.

Use branded hashtags, logos, colors, and imagery to reinforce your organization's identity and increase brand recognition.

Implementing Effective Social Media Tactics

3.1 Building and Growing Your Community

Cultivate an engaged and supportive community of followers, supporters, donors, and advocates on social media.

Encourage participation, interaction, and user-generated content to foster a sense of belonging and ownership among your audience.

3.2 Engaging with Your Audience

Actively engage with your audience by responding to comments,

messages, and mentions in a timely and personalized manner.
Initiate conversations, polls, Q&A sessions, and live streams to spark dialogue, solicit feedback, and build relationships with your community.

3.3 Leveraging Visual Storytelling

Harness the power of visual storytelling to effectively convey your nonprofit's mission, impact, and success stories.
Share compelling photos, videos, infographics, and testimonials that evoke emotion, inspire action, and drive engagement.

3.4 Amplifying Your Reach with Paid Advertising

Explore paid advertising options on social media platforms, such as Facebook Ads, Instagram Ads, and LinkedIn Sponsored Content, to expand your reach and visibility.
Set clear objectives, target audience parameters, and budget allocations to maximize the effectiveness of your paid advertising campaigns.

Measuring and Evaluating Performance

4.1 Tracking Key Metrics and Analytics

Monitor and analyze key metrics and analytics to assess the performance and impact of your social media efforts.
Evaluate engagement metrics, reach, impressions, conversions, and other relevant KPIs to measure success and identify areas for improvement.

4.2 Using Insights to Inform Strategy

Use social media insights, analytics tools, and data-driven insights to inform your social media strategy and decision-making.
Identify trends, patterns, and audience preferences to optimize content, timing, and tactics for maximum impact and effectiveness.

Staying Up to Date with Trends and Best Practices

5.1 Continuous Learning and Adaptation

Stay informed about emerging trends, innovations, and best practices in social media marketing for nonprofits.

Attend conferences, webinars, and training sessions, and follow industry experts and thought leaders to stay ahead of the curve.

5.2 Experimentation and Innovation

Embrace a culture of experimentation and innovation by testing new content formats, engagement tactics, and platform features. Iterate, refine, and adapt your social media strategy based on feedback, results, and evolving audience preferences.

Conclusion and Action Plan

6.1 Recap of Key Takeaways

Summarize the key strategies, tactics, and best practices covered in this guide for promoting your nonprofit on social media.

Highlight the importance of consistency, authenticity, and engagement in building your organization's successful social media presence.

6.2 Action Plan for Implementation

Develop an action plan outlining specific steps, timelines, and responsibilities for implementing the strategies and cs discussed in this g

Set realistic goals, benchmarks, and milestones to measure progress and the success of your social media efforts over

By following this comprehensive guide and implementing the strategies outlined, your nonprofit organization can effectively leverage social media to raise awareness, attract supporters, and drive action for your mission. With dedication, creativity, and strategic planning, you can harness the full potential of social media to make a positive impact in your community and beyond.

CHAPTER 18

You can connect your nonprofit organization with your state house and federal government.

Connecting your nonprofit organization with your state house and federal government is essential for advocating for your cause, influencing policy decisions, and accessing resources and support. In this comprehensive guide, we'll explore step-by-step strategies and best practices for establishing and nurturing relationships with state and federal government officials.

Understanding the Importance of Government Relations

1.1 Advocating for Your Cause

Learn why government relations are crucial for nonprofits, including the ability to advocate for policy changes, funding opportunities, and regulatory support.

Understand the role of government officials, agencies, and committees in shaping legislation and decision-making processes.

1.2 Accessing Resources and Support

Explore the potential benefits of connecting your nonprofit with government entities, including access to grants, contracts, technical assistance, and collaborative opportunities.

Understand how government partnerships can enhance your

organization's capacity, credibility, and impact on the community.

Identifying Key Stakeholders and Decision-Makers
2.1 Researching Government Officials
Conduct research to identify key government officials, representatives, senators, and agencies at both the state and federal levels.
Gather information about their backgrounds, roles, priorities, and contact details using online resources, directories, and databases.
2.2 Mapping Decision-Making Processes
Understand the legislative and regulatory processes at the state house and federal government levels, including how bills are introduced, debated, and enacted into law.
Identify relevant committees, hearings, and public forums where you can engage with government officials and advocate for your nonprofit's interests.

Building Relationships and Engaging with Government Officials
3.1 Establishing Initial Contact
Introduce your nonprofit to government officials through personalized emails, letters, or phone calls, expressing your organization's mission, goals, and areas of mutual interest.
Request meetings, briefings, or site visits to provide government officials with firsthand insight into your organization's work and impact.
3.2 Cultivating Relationships
Build and nurture relationships with government officials through regular communication, updates, and engagement opportunities.
Demonstrate your organization's credibility, expertise, and commitment to community service through collaborative initiatives and shared outcomes.

Advocating for Policy Change and Funding Opportunities
4.1 Developing Advocacy Campaigns
Identify policy issues, legislative proposals, or budget priorities aligning with your nonprofit's mission.

Develop advocacy campaigns, messaging, and strategies to educate and mobilize government officials, stakeholders, and the public around your advocacy goals.

4.2 Engaging in Legislative and Regulatory Processes

Monitor legislative and regulatory developments that impact your nonprofit's work and advocate for policy changes or amendments as needed.

Participate in hearings, town halls, and public comment periods to provide input, testimony, and feedback on proposed legislation or regulations.

Accessing Grants, Contracts, and Technical Assistance

5.1 Researching Funding Opportunities

Explore grants, contracts, and technical assistance programs offered by government agencies, departments, and initiatives at the state and federal levels.

Use online databases, grant portals, and funding announcements to identify relevant opportunities for your nonprofit.

5.2 Building Grant-Writing and Contracting Capacity

Develop grant-writing and contracting capacity within your nonprofit by training staff, volunteers, or consultants on proposal development, budgeting, and compliance.

Seek technical assistance, workshops, or webinars offered by government agencies or nonprofit organizations to enhance your skills and knowledge in grant-seeking and management.

Leveraging Coalitions and Partnerships

6.1 Forming Coalitions and Alliances

Collaborate with other nonprofits, advocacy groups, coalitions, and community organizations to amplify your collective voice and advocacy efforts.

Identify shared priorities, common goals, and areas of collaboration that can strengthen your advocacy impact and influence.

6.2 Engaging in Public Policy Networks

Join public policy networks, advocacy coalitions, and professional associations that advocate for specific policy issues or sectors relevant to your nonprofit's mission.

Participate in meetings, conferences, and advocacy days to network with peers, share best practices, and coordinate advocacy strategies at the state and federal levels.

Advocating for Diversity, Equity, and Inclusion

7.1 Prioritizing Diversity, Equity, and Inclusion

Integrate diversity, equity, and inclusion principles into your nonprofit's advocacy efforts, policies, and practices.

Advocate for policies, programs, and funding opportunities that promote equity, address systemic disparities, and advance social justice in your community.

7.2 Building Coalitions and Partnerships

Collaborate with diverse stakeholders, communities, and organizations representing marginalized or underrepresented populations in your advocacy efforts.

Amplify the voices and perspectives of those most affected by social and economic inequities in your advocacy campaigns and policy priorities.

Evaluating and Monitoring Advocacy Impact

8.1 Tracking Advocacy Efforts

Monitor and evaluate the impact of your advocacy efforts through key performance indicators (KPIs), metrics, and outcomes.

Track legislative outcomes, policy changes, funding allocations, and other indicators of success to assess.

CHAPTER 19

The Significance of Establishing a Nonprofit Organization with a 501(c) Tax-Exempt Certificate

Establishing a nonprofit organization with a 501(c) tax-exempt certificate signifies more than a bureaucratic requirement; it embodies a strategic decision with profound implications for its mission, sustainability, and impact. This comprehensive exploration delves into the importance of obtaining this coveted status and its myriad benefits to nonprofit entities and the communities they serve.

Understanding the 501(c) Tax-Exempt Status

1.1 Defining a 501(c) Tax-Exempt Certificate:
The Internal Revenue Service (IRS) grants 501(c) tax-exempt status.
This section explains the eligibility criteria and requirements for obtaining this designation.
1.2 Exploring Legal and Financial Implications:
It discusses the legal and financial benefits associated with 501(c) status, including exemption from federal income tax, eligibility for public and private grants, and tax-deductible contributions for donors.

Advantages for Nonprofit Organizations

2.1 Enhancing Credibility and Trust:
This paper explores how 501(c) status enhances an organization's credibility, legitimacy, and transparency in the eyes of donors, stakeholders, and the public.

2.2 Accessing Funding Opportunities:
This paper examines the diverse funding opportunities available exclusively to 501(c) organizations, including government grants, foundation grants, and corporate sponsorships.

2.3 Tax Benefits for Donors:
Analyzes the tax benefits enjoyed by donors who contribute to 501(c) organizations, such as deductions for charitable contributions and potential reductions in estate taxes.

Impact on Mission Fulfillment

3.1 Focusing on Mission-driven Activities:
This paper explores how 501(c) status allows nonprofit organizations to focus on their mission-driven activities without the burden of federal income tax obligations.

3.2 Ensuring Long-term Sustainability:
Examines how tax-exempt status facilitates long-term sustainability by providing financial stability, reducing operational costs, and attracting ongoing support from donors and funders.

Community and Social Impact

4.1 Strengthening Community Engagement:
Discusses how tax-exempt nonprofits are better positioned to engage with their communities, mobilize resources, and effectively address pressing social issues.

4.2 Amplifying Social Impact:
Analyzes the significant social impact tax-exempt nonprofit organizations can achieve through their programs, services, and advocacy efforts.

Compliance and Accountability

5.1 Ensuring Regulatory Compliance:
Provides an overview of the compliance requirements and

reporting obligations associated with 501(c) status, including the annual filing of Form 990 with the IRS.

5.2 Promoting Transparency and Accountability:

Examines how tax-exempt organizations are held to higher transparency and accountability standards, fostering stakeholder trust and confidence.

Challenges and Considerations

6.1 Managing Administrative Burdens:

Discusses the administrative burdens associated with obtaining and maintaining 501(c) status, including the application process, record-keeping requirements, and compliance with IRS regulations.

6.2 Navigating Restrictions on Activities:

This paper examines the constraints and regulations enforced on tax-exempt organizations, including prohibitions on engaging in political lobbying and partisan activities.

Conclusion and Recommendations

7.1 Recap of Key Findings:

Summarizes the key benefits, challenges, and considerations of establishing a nonprofit organization with a 501(c) tax-exempt certificate.

7.2 Providing Recommendations for Nonprofit Leaders:

This guide offers practical recommendations and best practices for nonprofit leaders seeking to leverage the advantages of 501(c) status to advance their mission and maximize their impact.

In conclusion, the importance of obtaining a 501(c) tax-exempt certificate for nonprofit organizations cannot be overstated. Beyond the legal and financial benefits, tax-exempt status confers credibility, enhances transparency, and facilitates community engagement, enabling nonprofits to fulfill their missions and create lasting social change. While challenges and compliance requirements exist, the rewards far outweigh the drawbacks, making 501(c) status an indispensable asset for any nonprofit committed to making a positive difference.

CHAPTER 20

The intricate process of establishing, operating, and promoting a nonprofit organization focuses on the United States context, with particular emphasis on Atlanta, Georgia.

In this guide, we have delved into the intricate process of establishing, operating, and promoting a nonprofit organization. We have focused on the context of the United States, with particular emphasis on Atlanta, Georgia. From defining the mission and vision to navigating legal requirements, engaging with government entities, and leveraging social media for visibility, we have provided a thorough exploration of the key steps and strategies involved in nonprofit management.

We began by emphasizing the importance of careful planning, research, and consultation with professionals to ensure legal and regulatory requirements compliance. From there, we discussed the significance of crafting a compelling mission and vision statement, developing bylaws, and forming a board of directors to effectively guide the organization's operations.

We explored the process of incorporating a nonprofit in detail, including the necessary steps, such as choosing a name, filing articles of incorporation, obtaining an Employer Identification Number (EIN), and registering for tax-exempt status.

Additionally, we highlighted the importance of maintaining accurate records and filing annual reports to comply with state and federal regulations.

Building visibility and promoting the nonprofit were also key topics of discussion. We explored strategies for creating a professional website, leveraging social media platforms, engaging with influencers and partners, participating in community events, and cultivating relationships with media outlets to raise awareness and attract support for the organization's mission.

Moreover, we emphasized the importance of government relations in advocating for policy change, accessing funding opportunities, and amplifying the nonprofit's impact. By establishing connections with government officials at the state and federal levels, nonprofits can effectively influence decision-making processes and access valuable resources to support their work.

This guide emphasized the value of continuous learning, adaptation, and collaboration in nonprofit management. By staying informed about emerging trends, best practices, and opportunities for innovation, nonprofits can adapt their strategies to maximize their impact and achieve their organizational goals.

CHAPTER 21

Epilogue:

As we conclude this comprehensive guide to nonprofit management, the journey of building and sustaining a nonprofit organization is both challenging and rewarding. From the initial stages of defining the mission and incorporating the organization to promoting visibility, engaging with stakeholders, and advocating for change, nonprofits play a vital role in addressing pressing social issues and positively impacting our communities.

We hope that the insights, strategies, and resources shared in this guide will empower nonprofit leaders, volunteers, and supporters to navigate the complexities of nonprofit management with confidence and clarity. By embracing innovation, collaboration, and a commitment to social change, nonprofits can overcome challenges, seize opportunities, and fulfill their missions to create a better world.

As we look ahead to the future, let us continue to work together to build stronger, more resilient communities where every individual could thrive and contribute to positive social change. Thank you for your dedication, passion, and tireless efforts to make a difference through your nonprofit organization. Together, we can create a brighter future for generations to come.

ABOUT THE AUTHOR

Juliana Michael

Other Books by This Author
The Mystery Behind the Wind
From Writer to Wealth: Mastering Publishing Like A PRO on Amazon

Made in the USA
Columbia, SC
13 June 2024